Social Movements

FOR GOOD

How Companies and Causes Create Viral Change

DERRICK FELDMANN

WILEY

Published by John Wiley & Sons, Inc., Hoboken, New Jersey.
Published simultaneously in Canada.

For general information about our other products and services, please contact our Customer Care Department within the United States at (800) 762-2974, outside the United States at (317) 572-3993, or fax (317) 572-4002.

Wiley publishes in a variety of print and electronic formats and by print-on-demand. Some material included with standard print versions of this book may not be included in e-books or in print-on-demand. If this book refers to media such as a CD or DVD that is not included in the version you purchased, you may download this material at http://booksupport.wiley.com. For more information about Wiley products, visit www.wiley.com.

Library of Congress Cataloging-in-Publication Data:

Names: Feldmann, Derrick, 1978–
Title: Social movements for good: how companies and causes create viral change / Derrick Feldmann.
Description: Hoboken : Wiley, 2016. | Includes bibliographical references and index.
Identifiers: LCCN 2015039889 (print) | LCCN 2015042192 (ebook) |
   ISBN 978-1-119-13339-1 (hardback) | ISBN 978-1-119-13340-7 (pdf) |
   ISBN 978-1-119-13342-1 (epub)
Subjects: LCSH: Social movements. | Leadership. | Nonprofit organizations. |
   BISAC: BUSINESS & ECONOMICS / Nonprofit Organizations & Charities.
Classification: LCC HM881 .F445 2016 (print) | LCC HM881 (ebook) |
   DDC 303.48/4—dc23
LC record available at http://lccn.loc.gov/2015039889

Cover Image: © iStock.com/JOZZ
Cover Design: Wiley

Printed in the United States of America.

10 9 8 7 6 5 4 3 2 1

To Paige and Blair, I can't wait to see how you will change this world for the better.

To Bis, who has been with me on this adventure for more than 10 years.

Contents

Preface

The date was May 25, 1986. I was eight years old. My mom and dad came into my room to take our family to Springfield, Illinois, for something called Hands Across America. Traveling 100 miles in the family car, I knew nothing about what we were going to do, be a part of, or even what it was for.

That day, for 15 minutes, my dad, mom, sister, and I joined hands with more than 6.5 million other Americans across the country. We donated $10 to reserve our spot in line, and our donation, combined with others, raised more than $34 million to alleviate famine in Africa and fight hunger and homelessness in the United States.

This was my first social movement for good.

Looking back, I'm extremely thankful to my mom and dad for bringing me there. That experience influenced how I look at cause work and helped make me who I am today.

Social movements are very much a part of our culture. At some point, we have all participated in one of these movements—as donors, as activists, and as promoters of these important events that make

FIGURE P.1   Registering for Hands Across America with my Mother—Annette Feldmann

change happen. It's hard to ignore the many movements happening in our society. They enthrall us. Our friends and family care passionately about something and by virtue of our relationship, so do you. These movements matter.

From that summer day in 1986 when I joined hands with 6.5 million other individuals for Hands Across America to 2014's ALS Ice Bucket Challenge, I can't fully recall the number of movements that I have been part of or have touched my life.

Looking back and examining the movements I've participated in, I started to ask myself some questions. Why did I get so excited about that particular cause at that specific time? Why did I do something or take an action then that I would never think of doing now? Why did I donate money during that movement, and did it make a difference?

All of these questions that I started pondering combined with the questions about social movements I hear daily from fundraisers, nonprofit leaders, corporate executives, activists, and public servants have become the impetus for this book.

My team and I have spent the past six years researching how Millennials (individuals born from 1980 to 2000) get involved with causes and what factors trigger and influence their behavior. I realized it was time to look at social movements today to try to answer some of these questions. Rather than focus on one generation over another, I wanted to learn how and why these movements start and inspire so many people to participate in them.

This book examines social movements that have occurred in the past 10 years—movements that have inspired so many people to act for good, champion a cause, and build awareness for an issue. The goal of the book is to help organizations and companies, social movement builders, and entrepreneurs who share a common goal of inspiring others to act for good by providing them with the stories, people, approaches, and strategies for successful social movement building. My hope is to provide the real context to the movements of today so that those who read this book can be compelled to change their methods and cultivate successful movements of their own.

Of course, the first thing you should know is that every social movement is unique. No relevant social movement can fully mirror one from the past. Because movements are about people and not a theory and approach, it's the people who drive the agenda, outcome, and success. Therefore, this book is not intended to be an outline of a path but rather a descriptor of what has been proven to work for so many leaders who have forged the road ahead to create social movements that address important issues in our communities, our country, and our world.

You may be wondering *why*.

Why study movements at all?

Social movements represent a pure opportunity for change. Movements unite us. And sometimes movements even divide us. But the movements that are built by a community of people who believe in the same thing have one goal/serve a purpose: to help themselves and others like them, or to help those they may never meet but want to ensure they have opportunities like them. These movements represent the causes shaping our society and what we describe as "good."

Every organization in the world wants to create a movement behind their brand, cause, or product. But not everyone will get the opportunity—or, quite honestly, should—if they aren't willing to embed within their movement building the common characteristics of social movements for good. Essentially, understanding how the social movement builders of today have been successful will help those that aspire to lead people from cause enthusiasts to cause activists and beyond.

This book opens with a review of what constitutes a "social movement for good." I compare "movements for good" to other movements to clarify the types of movements discussed throughout the book. I also want to talk about empathy and the role it plays in our society and individual response to social movements.

Following each chapter you will see a "viewpoint" from a social movement builder who I spent some time with. The purpose of each viewpoint is to see how one person was able to create and ignite the movement he or she built, what he or she learned, and what advice he or she would offer individuals interested in creating a movement on their own. The viewpoints are also based on the time we (myself and my research team at Achieve) spent looking at social movements objectively. This research enabled us to approach each social movement builder with a series of in-depth questions that led to the viewpoint and profile in this book.

As you'll see, the third chapter is focused on the challenges most social movement builders have with this kind of work to let the community own the movement and move to the side to allow the people the course and opportunity to make it their own. Chapters 4 and 5 focus on the marketing, narrative, and symbolism that are often tied to social movements in an effort to inspire action.

It is hard to ignore what companies are doing today to inspire social movements of their own. The companies profiled in this book go beyond checkbook philanthropy and focus on being part of the community that affects their customers and employees. Through business approaches focused on products and cause marketing to creating some of the unique programs for employees, Chapter 6 highlights the people who were the real pioneers of social movements for good through business.

Chapter 7 focuses on international social movements and why and how they have received so much traction in the United States, especially with younger demographics. The chapter also explores the international NGOs (nongovernmental organizations) that have been able to effectively show stories of inequality throughout the world to inspire action.

Chapter 8 highlights the creative approaches to some social movements. In this chapter, successful campaigns that have had successful responses from the public are highlighted in addition to their approach and strategy to reaching so many people through imagery, video, and other creative assets. The chapter also details the concepts and ideas behind the creative so as to reach movement status.

Chapter 9 focuses on collegiate-level social movements. More than 20 million young people attended college in 2015. Because of the sheer size of the population in college today, a great opportunity exists for organizations looking to build momentum around an issue. From dance marathons to on-campus organizing, this chapter covers how campus leaders are raising support and awareness for some of the biggest causes in the country.

Chapter 10 examines how most of the causes and companies highlighted in this book leverage peer engagement. From initial introductions to the resources offered, social movements use peers effectively to garner financial support for an issue.

Peer engagement also plays a huge role in how we share information, which led to the final chapter, Chapter 11, on hashtag activism. Using social networks to share concepts, ideas, and actions while attaching them to a common thread and network allows a social movement to build. However, we also cover in this chapter how hashtag activism needs certain components to be effective in tipping the network of people into a true movement.

As you embark upon your own personal journey of social movement building for good, remember a few of things:

First, social movement building is never about you and your personal achievements. Rather, it is always about the people who desire to create change for something bigger than what they are.

Second, social movement building requires resources, and not the ones you may be thinking about. Today's social movement builders often start with humble budgets, but an abundance of passion, drive, and an unquenchable thirst to enact change and solve a problem.

Third, social movement building is not equal to social networking. Social media is an opportunity for social movements to connect and grow, but it takes people involving with each other to maintain and build a real social movement for good.

Finally, social movement building for good isn't easy. There are a lot of causes, ideas, and marketing schemes that are vying for attention. And in all of that information out there for every regular person to see, hear, and feel, your movement for good could be buried. But don't give up. A movement needs people to spread it, and it will take every network and contact you have to be willing to share it with every network and contact they have. You may never get the viral traction you desire, but in the end, if any cause or company is able to bring anyone together for good, I think that is a noble idea and one worth celebrating.

So here's to social movements for good. People are waiting, so let's get started.

Acknowledgments

One of the truest statements I've heard came from Marc Roberge, front-man for the band O.A.R, at MCON 2015. During his onstage interview, he said that a friend of his has a tattoo that says **"I get to."** That statement pretty much sums up the journey I have been on for the last seven years—a journey that has been truly remarkable. And I owe this journey to so many people.

I get to work with some incredible people who remind me daily of the real reason why we do what we do for the field—to help others truly understand the reasons why people get involved to make a difference. These individuals include my team at Achieve—Clay Williams, Slade Sundar, Marianna Williams, Robert Anderson, Monte Lambert, and Jeremy Morse. And to my research and creative team, I can't put into words how much I appreciate the work of Amy Thayer, Natalie Clayton, and Hillary Celebi.

I want to especially thank four members of the Achieve team—Joey Ponce for his brilliant cover design, Jonathon Hosea and Hannah Lushin for their incredible editing skills, and Melissa Wall for her help with research and organizing all of these interviews—they were put to great use for this book project.

I get to meet great people while I travel on the road sharing the story of Millennials, social movements, and cause enthusiasts waiting to take action for an issue they care about. From New Zealand to Saskatchewan, I've had the opportunity to visit, see, and meet passionate people across the globe. I can't thank Celeste Franklin enough for helping to manage my time and speaking engagements.

I get to collaborate with individuals who are helping the world understand this space of "doing good" a little better. From the wonderful team at Wiley, including Matthew Davis and Alyssa Beningo, to the team at *Philanthropy News Digest* of the Foundation Center, Emily Robbins and Mitchell Nauffts, that have allowed me to take my ideas, research, and thoughts to another level.

I get to interview some remarkable people who are truly making a difference in the world of causes and social good. Some of their stories I have shared in this book, including Adam Braun, James Coan, Azita Ardakani, Jay Coen Gilbert, Kim Jordan, Shea Parton, Raan Parton, Joe Rospar, Scott Harrison, and Mallory Brown. Thank you for your time and willingness to be a part of this book project.

I get to partner with some incredible organizations that have made a difference in how I think about cause engagement and the work that we do. I want to say a special thanks to the Case Foundation, Jean Case, Emily Yu, and the rest of the team who have been instrumental in bringing to light the opportunity Millennials and entrepreneurs have to make real change.

I get to meet regularly and gain valuable advice from true pioneers in their respective fields. I am forever grateful to Clay Robbins, Ted Grossnickle, Dorothy (Dottie) Johnson, Robert Collier, Kathy Agard, Robert Whitacre, Rachel Hutchinson, Andrew Watt, and Diana Aviv. Thank you for your willingness to listen and guide me in my thinking.

Finally, I get to be Bis's husband and Paige and Blair's dad. A true honor that I cherish every day and one that moves me more than they will ever realize.

About the Author

Derrick Feldmann is a sought-after speaker, researcher, and adviser in cause engagement. He founded Achieve to help organizations address their most pressing issues through research and data-driven, strategically designed fundraising and awareness campaigns.

Derrick is the lead researcher and creator of the Millennial Impact Project, a multiyear study of how the next generation supports causes. This ongoing study has been cited in hundreds of publications, including *Forbes, TIME, Fast Company, The Chronicle of Philanthropy,* the *Wall Street Journal,* and the *New York Times.* Through this research, as well as in his role at Achieve, Derrick has worked with companies and organizations such as AT&T, Facebook, BMW, PBS, and the Case Foundation to understand how the next generation of donors, activists, and employees are redefining cause work.

He is the founder of MCON, the nation's premier conference on Millennials and social good, which draws speakers from for- and nonprofit organizations across the world. MCON explores the question of whether and how organizations are taking advantage of today's heightened interest in causes to better serve their constituents.

Derrick is also the co-author of the book *Cause for Change: The Why and How of Nonprofit Millennial Engagement* (2012). He is also a regular contributor to *Philanthropy News Digest* and the Huffington Post IMPACT channel. He is on the Leadership Faculty of the Points of Light Corporate Institute, a guest lecturer for the School of Public and Environmental Affairs at Indiana University.

He received an undergraduate degree from Southeast Missouri State University and a graduate degree from the Lilly Family School of Philanthropy at Indiana University. He went on to lead national fundraising efforts for The LEAGUE and Learning to Give before founding Achieve in 2008.

Derrick lives in Indianapolis with his wife, Bis, and their two daughters.

Chapter 1   The Movement for Good

I grew up in a town of 1,000 people in southern Illinois. As the saying goes, "everyone knows everyone," and the people who reside there believe in the importance of looking out for one's neighbor. You support them when times are tough—maybe not always with money, but with time, emotional support, food, and whatever else you can offer.

In the area where I grew up, the belief in helping someone close to you was rooted in deep tradition. You stand up for people in need. You know them personally, you care deeply, and you build relationships with the people surrounding the families. There is something to be said about rural philanthropy and contributing to a community when you know the beneficiary personally.

This is how I grew up. This was my perception of philanthropy and the way the world worked. If someone needed help, you stepped in. If someone experienced a tragedy, you were on call.

As I grew up and left this small town in Illinois, I noticed things were slightly different in the rest of the world.

I traveled to cities and took jobs in philanthropy. To my surprise, people would help those they *didn't* necessarily know personally. They would react to a story, a symbol, and a dream of what life could be. Not someone they knew.

Early into my first job in fundraising I realized I was taking on the role of storyteller—the one conveying the hurt to those able to make it possible. I was the one who made the issue, the need, the pain come to life. And I was responsible for getting people to act. Whether it was a $10 donation or a $10,000 donation, I was the one who made the story of need relevant.

As an analytical person, at times I would ask myself: *How is it possible that someone can react and be a part of something when they don't know the people involved?*

How is it that thousands of people can be moved when a call comes out about an issue or a family or even an injustice when they weren't a part of it?

It is an interesting point to think about. Do you ever wonder how so many people could participate with a group of people they don't know, had never met, and had little experience with the issue?

It took me a while, but I finally figured it out. These individuals, including myself at times, would participate in efforts that we will call *movements* because those who can't stand up for themselves need the voices of strangers to be there for them. We as individuals are tied to the emotional need and support of such a group of people that it is necessary for those who will never experience the cause or touch the hand of a person in need to rise above and be vocal on their behalf. Because they believed in the power of adding their voice, action, and support to the cause, all in the hope that someone, somewhere will hear it. And because of their action, the unknown and the uneducated will hear, act, and ultimately attach themselves to the same cause.

Some would say this seems like wishful thinking. But in reality it is the thinking of a powerful citizenry that's ready to make the plight of others known, and take meaningful action.

That is the power of social movements for good.

We forget at times how rational we are, how we are humans.

We are a race of humans and emotions. Seeking to validate, participate, and lift up those who we think need such actions.

Social movements for good is a defining moment in time in which people, beyond those affected, believe in the power of the issue that affects those who need a voice. They rise up with others to build the awareness and the clout necessary to transform an issue into a cause and a cause into a moment of inspiration.

Social movements for good are created because of the beneficiary *and* the need for the participant to fulfill their personal passion—a dual motivation that yields a powerful mechanism when leveraged among so many individuals.

I mention all of this because it is a belief that has been rooted in the way I perceive human and philanthropic behavior today.

In the preface to this book, I shared my personal experience with Hands Across America. I had no idea what I was doing or what holding hands meant for so many others. It was just a weird thing to me. A concept of showing, as my mom said to me, support for an issue I should care about. In fact, I don't even remember what the issue was.

This by far, was one of my first experiences growing up and participating in a social movement. Looking back now, 30 years later, I am still astonished at the power this social movement had on so many others and how my action that day meant something.

So what do these social movements say about us?

It's an interesting take on the role movements like these have for us. Some will say these movements build momentum. Others will say it is a flash in the dark for so many issues and causes to be had. Then why do we participate? Why do we gather, tell stories, and organize around a symbol or a sign of commitment?

That's what this book is about.

This book explores the reasons why we pour ice on our heads to show support for ALS, put a red nose on our face to fight hunger, or carry a puzzle piece with us to show our support for autism research.

It's the reason my mom told me to join hands with 6.5 million other people to make a difference.

Social movements are at the core of who we are as a society. Each year, we witness new emerging movements. Some take off, while others will die shortly, without a breath of air.

Before exploring social movements for good, let's explore what defines a movement.

DEFINING *MOVEMENTS*

The concept of a movement can take many forms. Some might say that the organization they work for is creating a movement to help people overcome a specific issue. Others will say the movement they are creating is more conceptual and doesn't need an organization to champion the work.

Although any injustice-, challenge-, or awareness-building effort can gain some traction, not all will reach the movement stage and reach a mass audience. Did you know that approximately 3,000 events and rallies occur at the National Mall in Washington, D.C. every year?[1] Given the amount of potential interests in issues and policies, every person who rallies and participates hopes that their participation in the movement they believe in will get the notoriety of media and the public. But not all do.

A movement is a group of people working together for a common social, political, or cultural goal. At times, the movement's focus can be an injustice, an opportunity for change, and even a promotion of a theory or concept. The movement requires a key element to make it move from an idea of a few to an idea of many: people. People play an important role in the movement building of today. People are needed to spread the word of the movement's success, recruit others to create a larger group, and build the infrastructure to maintain the movement over a period of time.

But that is where the movement begins to either grow into social movement status or wither. If you look at the most successful movements, the movement builders (leaders who are masterminds behind social organizing) create a movement that builds in importance for the public at large, a narrative of belief for the general public, and an onset of relevant and timely stories for the media to pay attention to. The unsuccessful movements of our time lack the relevancy for the general public to care, a broader story of challenge, a need to overcome that the media can report beyond a niche community facing struggle, and, most importantly, the felt need that the time for change is now. Therefore, the movement, while important, doesn't reach the mass scale of other social movements and will eventually fade as the impassioned organizers begin to see little traction beyond the initial phases of organization.

The term "social movement" was introduced in 1848 by the German sociologist Lorenz von Stein in his book *Socialist and Communist Movements since the Third French Revolution* (1848). Noted sociologists and scholars such as Charles Tilly define social movements as a series of contentious performances, displays, and campaigns by which ordinary people make collective claims on others. Another scholar, Sidney Tarrow, defines social movements as *collective challenges*

---

[1] http://dc.about.com/od/specialevents/tp/National-Mall-Events.htm.

[to elites, authorities, other groups, or cultural codes] by people with common purposes and solidarity in sustained interactions with elites, opponents, and authorities.

These definitions help us understand that social movements require a collective power beyond small-group organizing to build and sustain a long-term goal of change for an issue. The collective power must come from groups of people—those affected and those caring for those affected—who demonstrate to leaders, as well as those who believe otherwise at the local or federal level that change is necessary. This includes a large audience who is calling on those who have the power to act to, then, act.

SOCIAL MOVEMENTS VERSUS SOCIAL MOVEMENTS FOR GOOD

Some will wonder how a "social movement" and a "social movement for good" really differ. When does a social movement become a social movement for good?

In looking at how social movements are defined, most movements (not all) begin by a group of people noticing an issue they believe needs attention. As explained in Figure 1.1, social movements for good, the concept, is based on raising the awareness of an issue to generate support for the benefit of an aggrieved group. Support for this group grows until change is achieved. This won't happen, though, until society has stepped forward with the public's interest and support for the issue.

Social movements for good are also rooted in the idea of a group of people combining resources to make an issue more apparent and noteworthy, even though the outcome may not be realized through policy change, but rather through further individual support. Take the Movember movement, for example. The purpose of Movember is to increase the public's awareness of prostate cancer, to urge people to take personal action to detect prostate cancer, and ultimately change the discourse on the issue. Although policy change may be a long-term goal, the movement's purpose didn't start out with driving policy change, but rather individual change as a result of the movement generating viral attention.

Social movements for good create a narrative of action that can go beyond protest and awareness building. Social movements for good provide an opportunity for people to organize around the issue, volunteer in local communities where that issue may be prevalent, and draw

	Social Movements	Social Movements for Good
Goal	Generate policy or cultural change.	Generate awareness about an issue or population in need of support and resources.
Disruption	Disrupting public discourse in an effort to generate awareness.	Disrupting current behavior in an effort to take personal action onto themselves or for a group of people.
Time frame	Public attitudes and cultural change can be affected overnight and may take years to be realized.	Issues in social movements for good are long-term and require sustained action and support beyond years of awareness and activity.
Participants	Individuals who are inspired to action on behalf of a group of people like themselves or a disparate group that lacks the rights and abilities the participants have been afforded.	Individuals who see how personal action can change a course for themselves or someone else. As a result of their personal action, they are affected or the population they want to help is affected because of their resources and support.
Narrative	Story of inequality, lack of resources, or social standing due to an injustice. The story is based on a population that is rising or of significance and lacks the potential rights afforded the majority.	Story of general knowledge and relevance based on a lack of understanding of an issue and the people affected. Through awareness and personal support through various actions, an issue can be prevented or supported by the participant.

FIGURE 1.1   Comparison of Social Movements and Social Movements for Good

upon their own resources to affect change. Action to help the oppressed or those represented by the movement doesn't need a policy to change per se, but rather the attention and interest of a new group of people who were unaware the challenges were present and not that far removed from them.

Social movements for good help the individual realize the relevancy of an issue and how acting through several means can change the course of an affected individual. In contrast to social movements focused solely on injustice and policy change in the immediate term, social movements for good establish a platform of awareness, individual action, outcomes, and sustainable change beyond initial participation and triumph. A social movement for good is a long-term educational and action-driving platform that can withstand policy issues and builds the army necessary for support through time, talent, and resources.

WHY DO SOCIAL MOVEMENTS FOR GOOD MATTER?

Social movements for good establish a mass platform of action for a population. The social movement for good platform for an issue helps inform and cultivate the awareness necessary to help prevent an issue from affecting more people. Social movements for good have the power to generate awareness to produce results in areas such as public policy and healthcare. The social movement for good space is necessary to drive the preventable measures that help the general population live longer, productive, happier lives. For example, movements on drug prevention, cancer screenings, or tobacco cessation all provide a sense of preventable measures that the general public, once aware, can overcome. Taken in the form of public service announcements (PSAs), media engagement, and small personal actions, this type of social movement is based on individual awareness and personal action—potentially toward themselves or people close to them.

Social movements for good support the interests of a community whose lives are affected by an issue. This group of people is often unable to overcome this issue without the additional support of dedicated community activists and donors. These social movements bring attention to an issue because it concerns a mass of people so great they are hard to ignore. These people need support systems and resources they are unable to provide by themselves and have therefore created institutions built through public support. This type of movement aims to build research funds, fund schools, and support workforce education. In this case, the individuals themselves may not be personally affected, but they are drawn to the issue because of relevant messages and resonance with the people affected.

FOUR PHASES OF SOCIAL MOVEMENTS FOR GOOD

Social movements for good take a substantial amount of human capital to generate interest from the onset or gather people who share already established common interests. Typically, these movements begin to develop a starter audience or group of early adopters. This group then inspires additional followers to join the movement in fighting for an issue, generating awareness, or helping a population. From there, the group begins to accelerate through a sequence of public tools that build mass awareness and ultimately drive viral participation in an action or activity. This is the peak of the movement and what generates the general public's interest.

From here, the movement ideally maintains its positioning and sustains ongoing actions through awareness efforts, activities, and messages that detail the ever-growing success of the movement itself. Over time, the movement sustains its performance as an annual tool to generate further headway on the issue or support for the people. Benchmarks, as defined by the movement builder or leader, become achieved and the movement moves into a formal and sustained phase of development as a long-term solution of the issue and people affected. The final outcome is a cycle of generating and building interest, heightened participation, and sustained long-term growth. This is conceptually displayed in the four phases of how social movements for good develop and sustain over time.

Phase 1: Building and Gathering a Group of Believers

The first step in social good movement building is about creating a group of believers. This initial group of believers typically represents the following groups: early adopters, those already affected, small groups already organized for the cause, and immediate circles of influence represented by close friends, family, and peers. The social movement for good in the early phase is essentially a shell and structure for the already converted to convene for a common theme and concept of action.

At times, this phase can be very challenging for the movement builder. If various groups are being convened, they may represent common yet disparate views on the issue. The movement builder creates a major concept and theme, but must understand the smaller issues that niche audiences may have a particular interest in exploiting.

This happens when the issue may be broad, with specialized challenges affecting various populations within the issue. For example, autism involves a spectrum. Within that spectrum, there are certain behaviors and signs that develop in some people that do not display in others. Asperger's Syndrome, which falls on the spectrum, does not describe everyone with autism. This group of concerned advocates and parents may want to ensure that their story within the autism narrative is particularly highlighted to help them generate awareness and understanding.

Phase 2: Letting the People Take Action with One Another

In this phase, movement builders have developed the tools and resources needed to help those who are involved with the movement to get organized. Through actions like signing a petition, fundraising, and volunteering, the populace of the movement can take the crucial step to generate awareness and solicit the support of their peers.

At this phase, we begin to see small-group organizing take shape. Small groups begin to form geographically and through shared connections to the issue. In addition, we begin to see the formations of leadership take shape within communities. These leaders, whether through formal or informal roles, begin to focus their energy on supporting the various groups forming around the issue. They will provide institutional and organizational support to each small group, become a bridge for the movement builder, and craft the localized message or approach for the movement in the niche group they represent.

Localized goals and outcomes that support the larger national benchmarks are beginning to take shape. The movement's outcomes as defined by a combination of support from the local and national efforts are determined through leaders working with various small groups and creating easily identifiable and achievable actions. In the end, goals and benchmarks once seen as unattainable are now closer and closer to the broad goal of mass awareness and participation.

During this phase, individuals begin to help spread the word though the use of online tools and advocacy efforts. Platforms such as Twitter, Facebook, and Change.org attract followers and help ignite the beginning of a social movement. Through organized activities, local groups and organizers help the unconverted understand how the issue affects them personally and locally, draw that attention to take an action, and spread the message.

Phase 3: The Pinnacle Action

After gathering like-minded individuals, people close to and affected by the issue as well as movement builders create a pinnacle action to draw viral participation by the general public. Although momentum for the issue is growing, a notable awareness builder along with meaningful action is still necessary to draw in the vast majority of the general public that has yet to hear or understand the issue.

The pinnacle action is a concerted action taken by the mass public to show support for the social movement for good. This action, either done personally or in concert with others, allows networks to share in the expression all while delivering an educational sign to others that the issue matters to them and should be of the utmost importance to those around them.

The pinnacle action can take many forms. These forms can represent symbols, actions, activities, and events. Each one, in and of itself, helps the community become aware of the issue. The social movements for good that have built a viral audience tend to rally around a symbol or activity that is performed by oneself so as to stand out from the crowd. Whether it is wearing a shirt, changing a profile image in social media, or deciding to grow facial hair, all actions are outwardly focused to networks and groups of people in an effort to drive attention to the outlier.

Once the converted and small groups perform the action, what next needs to be done is to go viral through social media to elevate and deliver the narrative to those that have not yet been exposed to the story. The media takes the story of the few who are working for a social movement for good to the public and drives ongoing action by others. This is supported by social media sharing, storytelling through new small groups, and nontraditional media such as blogs and personal platforms. The result is a new mass of individuals intentionally acting on behalf of those affected or themselves. The social movement for good is born and now has reached a level of importance in everyday interests.

Phase 4: Sustaining the Movement

After the pinnacle action and the story in the media is beginning to dwindle, the movement builders focus on the sustained importance of the social movement for good. This means the movement needs to move from one-time actions to consistent actions for the population served. Movement builders at this phase create platforms to move from initial action taken in the pinnacle action phase to ongoing sustained support. This is done through a series of various activism and fundraising approaches.

Movement builders will create steps for activism to convert cause enthusiasts to sustained cause supporters. These steps increase in intensity but offer the individual a chance to elevate their knowledge while also taking actions for the betterment of the population served. The steps can range from taking online activist support such as "liking" and sharing to offline engagements like organizing local events and meeting with local leaders and stakeholders. Each activism step gets the individual closer and closer to the issue while making them feel the movement is closer to achieving its said goal.

Movement builders also create steps to show and raise support for the issue. After the pinnacle action is created, the individual is brought through a series of communications to show how small gifts can lead to demonstrable change for the individual. A common tactic is to bring the individual in at small levels to show how such dollars can provide tangible goods and services to the ones affected, resulting in small giving by the participant. By showing how financial support and fundraising dollars can make an additional impact beyond activism, the movement builder creates a story of the need to take holistic action for the issue and thus funds are now needed to sustain the movement in the long term. At this stage, a case for support is created with a relevant narrative that will inform the individual of how each and every dollar can affect the individual and keep the movement going. By building a new story each time the individual provides financial support, the movement builder is able to carry on a message of hope and change and how both the action and financial resources of the movement participant have affected individual people.

In the sustaining phase, the movement builder begins to create ongoing campaigns that may draw in new audiences and actions. These annual campaigns, both fundraising and activism, provide a mechanism to reignite the interest of the past participants. Through marketing campaigns, individuals who initially reacted are educated on where the issue is today and how important it is to continue contributing. Through fundraising campaigns, past pinnacle action participants witness the collective power of dollars raised on a group of people and how their support can make the difference in just one individual. Each of these campaigns grows on each other and builds on the narrative delivered at the beginning of the social movement—take action and awareness for oneself and others—in the spirit of making a difference.

SOCIAL MOVEMENTS FOR GOOD—A NEW GENERATION OF ACTIVISM

Creating today's social movements is different from what it was like in the past. Today's social movements require narratives that can be easily shared—personally and digitally. Today's social movements are more challenged than ever to get to the viral stage given the rise in mass media outlets and the onslaught of shorter messages than ever before.

But what is exciting is that a new generation of activists in the United States is equipped with the interests and tools to join the movement builders of today. This generation of Millennials, born after 1980, have been supporting through their actions of giving their time, talent, and financial resources to causes they care about at astounding rates. Specifically, here are some facts from the Millennial Impact Project and Reports from 2010 to 2015 that speak to the power of this generation to participate in social movements:

- 93 percent of Millennials gave to nonprofit organizations in 2010, with 21 percent giving $1,000 or more during the course of the year, but the bulk of giving was distributed in small increments to many organizations (Millennial 2011).
- 85 percent of Millennials are motivated to give by a compelling mission or cause, and 56 percent by a personal connection or trust in the leadership of the organization (2011).
- Millennials are influenced by the decisions and behaviors of their peers.
- Millennials support issues rather than organizations.
- Nearly 70 percent of Millennials surveyed are willing to raise money on behalf of a nonprofit they care about (2013).
- By a margin of more than two to one, Millennials who volunteer for nonprofits are more likely to make donations (2012).
- 87 percent felt encouraged to volunteer or participate in their company's cause work and community initiatives (2014).
- In the past year, respondents took one or more of the following actions as a result of an email request: signed a petition or pledge (52 percent), donated (52 percent), and shared or forwarded news or updates (49 percent) (2013).
- Nearly three-quarters of respondents said they would tell Facebook friends about great nonprofit events, 68 percent said they would tell friends about impressive statistics about a cause or issue, and 65 percent said they would promote a nonprofit's great story or accomplishment. In addition, 61 percent said they would use Facebook to alert friends to volunteering opportunities and needs (2012).

Today, we have the population ready, so now more than ever is the right time for movement builders to build momentum, make their mark in history, and sustain the issue with the general public. This book will help those who have just created institutions, have formulated ideas, and have organized a group of people around a common purpose understand how social movements for good have been created and sustained in the eyes of the general public.

This book will share stories from both sides—the movement builders and the participants. It is a collection of observations from these two important social movement pillars. This book discusses the intention, strategy, and outcome the movement builders were able to create with their social movements for good. We will also highlight the stories of regular people participating in the movements. We will showcase what they think about the movement, the message, the meaning, and where they are now in the movement's phases of growth.

Now is the time to create, act, and move—what better way to create the social movements of tomorrow than by understanding the success of yesterday's social movements for good. It is time to build and to start a social movement for good.

Chapter 2 Empathy

"I would never support an issue just because. There has to be a reason and I seek the impact of the cause before showing any support." She later made a donation to a cause after seeing an image of a person in need.

—31-year-old female donor

A friend of mine is on the board of directors for a local nonprofit organization. In the fall of 2014, I got an email from him inviting me to the organization's gala. I get a lot of these kinds of invitations. In fact, I think I could go to one every weekend if I opened my calendar up.

The subject line to the email was great. It said: "I know you hate these things—but humor me." His first line is even better. "I get this is the kind of request that makes you want to run and hide, jump off a cliff, or better yet go in for a root canal. But I would love it if you could come to the event."

Here were the three reasons he said I should go:

1. I could hang out with him and his wife for the evening—good food and drinks.
2. There was going to be some fun entertainment.
3. We could hear about a cause and issue he is passionate about.

How could I say no?

At the event, they did something so many nonprofit galas have. A moment when they ask those in the audience to support the organization's work helping to alleviate homelessness locally. I knew it was coming. And so did my wife—since she was a former nonprofit executive at one time. I whispered to her, here we go. My friend comes up to me and says, "I don't expect you to give anything—just glad you are here." Whew, that was great because my intention wasn't to give at all. I was primarily here to see my friend and make sure I check off number one and two of his three reasons I should go.

As we were sitting at the table, someone—I suspect a staff person working for the organization—comes around and provides my wife and me with a pledge card and a small pencil. And magically, there was a bucket that appeared in the middle of the table—sitting empty, waiting for me and others to just drop our pledge cards in it. This was a sign of persuasive peer engagement that I have studied for years. And that is when I told myself, I suspect you have said the same thing at some point when you have been in similar situations, that whatever they say, I am not giving anything. This cause, although important, is not one of the designated issues that I am passionate about.

At this time I am looking around the room and I notice that everyone is pretty quiet, but there is a lot of small chatter. All of them are talking with their guests, spouses, partners, and loved ones about what we are about to experience. I can hear my other friend next to me tell his spouse, "We are not giving anything. You kind of went overboard on the credit card bill this month." To the right of my wife, another couple we know is talking quietly together but just loud enough that I can hear what's going on. She asks him, "How much should we give? I mean what is enough so it doesn't look like we are cheap. We need to support his cause, right?"

While this is going on, my wife and I are just smiling, because this is an environment we are so used to. We started our careers in the nonprofit sector, received a Master's of Arts in Philanthropy from Indiana University's School of Philanthropy, and have played a role either organizing or assisting in some way to raise support or awareness for similar events when we worked for organizations. She whispers in my ear, "Please don't be cheap or overanalyze this situation. Give some money." Well, that was not what I expected either. I mean do I really overanalyze these events?

Now was the moment. The room goes dark and then an image of a person comes on the screen. The individual clearly has no home and is malnourished. The individual on stage talks about the story of this individual in the image. The story is one we have heard before. The individual doesn't have a home because of a foreclosure scenario during the financial downturn in 2008. She lost her job a year later and took to the streets in an effort to live and find shelter. Then a new image comes on the screen. She is now present with two children. The individual on stage shares that she has two children living with her. At that moment, you can hear individuals gasp. My wife squeezes my hand and I can see she is emotionally touched. So are others at our table. Some are beginning to tear up. Others are fiddling with drinks at the table or what they are wearing to try to avoid letting their emotions overcome them.

After that last image, the lights come on and on stage is the individual we saw in the pictures. Looking healthy, safe, and calm. Not at all what we just witnessed. She shares the struggles and pain she went through and how the organization we were here to support helped her. Her children then came up on stage toward the end and the crowd rose from its seats.

Then a volunteer comes on stage to ask everyone at their tables to support the issue of homelessness and the work of the organization. I look across the table and everyone is working on their forms. People are getting out checkbooks, credit cards, and checking for how much cash they have on hand. Then everyone starts to put their cards in the bucket in the center of the table. My wife then says to me, "We really need to support this organization. They are doing incredible things. Did you see how they helped that family?"

We gave that night, even though I, like so many others, were determined not to give or give just a small amount in support of the people who asked us to come to the event. The motivation we had moved away from the personal interest of helping out a friend to true altruism and philanthropy because of what we witnessed. We became empathetic for the plight of someone else and moved to make a difference through our support. We became a believer in the issue rather than a mere participant in a fundraising approach.

Why? How was this possible that we would participate in this manner? This can also be applied to a larger question that so many executives will ask me when I talk to them about why people do what they do for an issue even if they were never close to the issue before they were introduced.

The answer lies in the empathy we have for others because we are human.

WE ARE HUMAN

If you read anything about fundraising in the nonprofit sector, you will hear about individuals who respond in surveys and interviews that they want to see the "impact of their potential gifts" before giving. Even in the studies that we have performed, this is a common response by the public to what would inspire them to give or get them to give for the first time.

But just like my wife and our friends at the charity gala, these interested donors don't always follow along with what their original intentions or predisposed ideas about how and why they would act. The individual, although clearly trying to apply more extensive philanthropic filters to their potential behavior, reacts because of empathy—a trait we as humans have for helping others.

Within social and psychological theory, there is the empathy-altruism hypothesis developed by Daniel Batson that states the following:

> The feelings of empathy for another person produce an altruistic motivation to increase that person's welfare .... The term *empathy* refers to feelings of compassion, sympathy, tenderness, and the like. Altruism refers to a motivational state in which the goal is to increase another person's welfare as an end in itself. (Altruistic acts are what are ordinarily called "good deeds.")[1]

When the theory came out, some argued against it. The reason for the disagreements was because, based on social theory from the past, all human behavior is based on more egocentric tendencies. This includes the acts and behaviors to help oneself before others, and that as humans,

---

[1] http://ericboonesarchi.sourceforge.net/Archive/Empathy-Altruism %20Hypothesis.pdf.

they shouldn't be concerned with helping others but rather focus on the welfare of themselves before others.

Some psychologists will argue, though, that even some altruistic behavior has some element of egoism built into the act. In essence, they would say that no altruistic act is completely pure of selfish interests. For example, these individuals would argue that the act of helping another person also helps the donor in some way. The individual receives some personal benefit of good feelings from their acts.

Either way, we know that humans are empathetic and have altruistic behavior—the interest and internalized traits to help those whose welfare may be at risk. But why does this happen at times and what triggers this? There is an interesting theory that this comes from a "common identity" that may exist within ourselves. Dr. Steve Taylor of Leeds Beckett University in the U.K. discusses this in an article from *Psychology Today*.

> It's this fundamental oneness which makes it possible for us to identify with other people, to sense their suffering and respond to it with altruistic acts. We can sense their suffering because, in a sense, we *are* them. And because of this common identity, we feel the urge to alleviate other people's—and to protect and promote their well-being—just as we would our own. In the words of the nineteenth-century German philosopher Schopenhauer, "My own true inner being actually exists in every living creature, as truly and immediately known as my own consciousness in myself ....This is the ground of compassion upon which all true, that is to say unselfish, virtue rests, and whose expression is in every good deed."[2]

Now that we realize part of our acts to help other people is based upon the empathetic and altruistic nature we have, let's see how this has been tested in various scenarios. In two specific cases, we can see this play out in research test environments with populations of individuals.

Researchers Batson et al. asked female students to take the place of "Elaine," who was receiving mild electric shocks. Those who were led to believe that a placebo drug they took

---

[2]https://www.psychologytoday.com/blog/out-the-darkness/201310/why-do-human-beings-do-good-things-the-puzzle-altruism.

led to empathetic concern offered to take the shocks whereas those who had been led to believe that they would feel distress were more likely to leave and not assist. In another study, Darley and Latané arranged a conversation over an intercom between students. The empathy-altruism model suggests that people are not always motivated to behave selfishly. One confederate said he suffered from seizures and later appeared to collapse. When participants thought they were the only listener, 85 percent helped; if there was one bystander, 62 percent helped; with four bystanders, 31 percent helped. It is worth noting that participants couldn't actually see if anyone else was helping.[3]

In each of the studies, the individual acted to help and provide support for another. The individual being challenged shared his or her plight through a story or scenario that inspired the individual to act on his or her behalf. This action, based on empathy and altruism is what makes the act of philanthropy (definition—for love of humankind) and social issue support one that is inherently built within the population. In essence, we are cause and social issue enthusiasts because of the empathy and altruism within us. We need someone, a social movement builder, organizer, and leader to bring it out.

DOES IMPACT MATTER?

As mentioned earlier, when an individual is asked within studies about his or her giving and service to a cause, there is no doubt the most consistent answer will be some mention about wanting to have the greatest impact with his or her gifts. He or she wants to know how the dollars will be spent, how it will be felt by the individual in need, and whether his or her gifts truly made a difference to the people who received support from the cause. In an ideal world, the individual would make every gift, every hour, truly count toward a cause and social issue.

But who wouldn't? Who wouldn't want to ensure that their support for a cause or the gifts of time spent on addressing the issue is put to good use? The question is leading in and of itself because the answer is

---

[3] www.revisionworld.com/a2-level-level-revision/psychology/social-psychology/altruism-and-bystander-behaviour.

undoubtedly going to be, "Yes, I would love to have an impact when I spend any time or money for a social issue." Do we really have people who would say, "Yes, I hope my gifts do nothing for a cause. I have so much discretionary money that I truly don't care how it is spent."

Then something magical happens when we are presented with an image and an individual's need to us. We call upon that empathetic trait we possess, and all of the filters we put in place, the comments we made about knowing an impact will happen before we give, starts to go away.

Here are examples of tests performed in the field with real donors and supporters that speak to the power of empathy in cause messages.

Example 1: Feeling Good

A study conducted by Michael Price of Georgia State University concluded that people enjoy the "warm glow" of giving and an empathetic message that can be used. He tested two messages in a campaign called Pick.Click.Give in Alaska. Alaskans are asked every year to apply for a Permanent Fund Dividend that comes from the state's mineral royalties. The fund allows Alaskans to give some of the payout they receive to a charity. The marketing campaign is called Pick.Click.Give.

Price tested two different messages to a group of Alaskans. The first message read as follows on a postcard:

Make Alaska Better

The second message, sent to a separate group, had the following message on the postcard:

Warm Your

The message with the "Warm Your Heart" concept had a higher response rate of more than 30 percent than the "Make Alaska Better" message from the same population sizes. Also, the amount of money contributed to the campaign was even higher. Those who gave through the "Warm Your Heart" message contributed 55 percent more than those who gave to the "Make Alaska Better" message. This meant that by simply changing the text in a message, charities and causes in Alaska could have received $1.5 million more.[4]

---

[4]http://spihub.org/site/resource_files/newsroom/2015_Advancing_Philanthropy.pdf.

In another study performed by psychologist Paul Slovic of the University of Oregon discovered that our empathy and emotion to help needs to focus on one rather than millions. During the study, Slovic and his team of researchers told a group of volunteers that a young girl was suffering from starvation and malnutrition. The story of the young girl suffering was followed with a request to see if they would be willing to help her. His research team then told a different group the same story of the girl who was suffering from starvation and malnutrition but changed the request a bit. This time, his team told the group that there are millions of others suffering just like her and asked them for support because a population needs them. Through the use of statistics and images, the second group of volunteers was told of the immense breadth of the issue.

The result? The second group of volunteers, the one shown information about the population suffering from starvation and malnutrition, along with statistics and a request to support the millions of people affected, gave half as much as the volunteer group that was exposed to the message of just the individual girl.[5]

As Slovic looked at this study and analyzed performance, he went on to make comments about how the human brain works that are important to note for any social movement builder. The following is an excerpt from an interview with NPR (National Public Radio) that aired on November 5, 2014.

> The volunteers in his study wanted to help the little girl because it would make them feel good and give them a warm glow. But when you mix in the statistics, volunteers might think that there are so many millions starving, "nothing I can do will make a big difference."
>
> Now if the human brain were a computer, the two conflicting feelings wouldn't cancel each other out. We would still help the little girl even if we couldn't help everyone. But the brain is a master at unconsciously integrating different feelings. So

---

[5] www.npr.org/sections/goatsandsoda/2014/11/05/361433850/why-your-brain-wants-to-help-one-child-in-need-but-not-millions.

the bad feeling diminishes the warm glow—and reduces the impulse to give generously to help the child.

In other words, people decline to do what they can do because they feel bad about what they can't do.[6]

This research tells us that part of the message contained an empathetic approach rather than simply relying on the donor to make a rational choice in giving. Although not purely altruistic, since the individual would receive a personal benefit of good feeling and personal passion, it brings home the point that for the vast majority of us, we will act emotionally and empathically when positioned with a message and concept from a cause or social issue.

HELPING MAKES ME HAPPY

Is it wrong to join a social movement because it makes you personally happy? This is a big question some may be wondering now that we have discussed the role of empathy and altruism and how it personally affects us. Let's first examine a little bit about what we know about the link between happiness and helping others.

A study was conducted by Dr. Harbaugh and his team of researchers at the University of Oregon to understand the theories and concepts of how it makes one personally feel when one supports an issue or cause. Although the experiment was focused on giving, one can get a sense of the realities of happiness one receives from being involved in social issues.

The research team recruited 19 women in Eugene, Oregon, and asked them to perform several different transactions. The transactions were recorded in a brain scanner that would ultimately tell how and why the transaction came through. They were also told that the research team would not know their personal transactions and decisions, therefore removing the social status of the experiment or outside influence one can exert upon subjects who have undergone some similar studies.

---

[6]www.npr.org/sections/goatsandsoda/2014/11/05/361433850/why-your-brain-wants-to-help-one-child-in-need-but-not-millions.

This was made possible by the brain scanner recording their choice and coding it with other actions and activity in the brain before any analysis occurred; therefore no indicators that identified the individual was possible.

Each of the 19 women was given $100 in an account that would be allocated to a local food bank in various increments. The women were given various choices and asked to make certain decisions based on their personal interests or altruistic inclinations. In some cases, they had an option to donate and in others they were subjected to certain "taxes" that would ultimately help the food make its way back through a citywide distribution model of funds.

Each participant in the study was presented with an amount of money on a screen. The amount could be $50 or $75 or some other amount that would test their response. After they were exposed to the dollar amount on the screen, they were later told that the amount was a gift to them, a tax in that amount, or they could donate such an amount to a local food bank. The individual, once asked, would need to make a decision to either accept or decline by pushing a button. After pushing the button, the brain scanner would look at the pleasure centers of the brain to determine which action had the most influence on the participant's happiness.

The results were overwhelming positive. All of the participants in the study, giving, receiving money, and taxation, produced positive feelings in the pleasure centers of the brain. This means that the act of supporting in some way gives us pleasure and is a positive internalized emotion that is caused by our actions. Some would ask, how is it possible that even taxation gives this feeling, too? Well, the individual was aware of how the tax would be used to help the charity or cause locally, similar to the other scenarios. It should be noted that giving to charity alone as a donation yielded the highest feelings of happiness and pleasure.[7]

One of the most comprehensive studies on happiness and doing good comes from Christian Smith and Hilary Davidson from their studies while leading the Science of Generosity Initiative at Notre Dame. They surveyed more than 2,000 individuals over a five-year period, performed a series of interviews, tracked spending habits and lifestyle

---

[7]https://www.psychologytoday.com/blog/the-compass-pleasure/201108/is-your-brain-charitable-giving.

changes and actions of 40 families from different economic classes and races in 12 states, and followed them as they participated in their daily life. The researchers even followed them to the grocery store.

The researchers found that performing generous acts makes us happy. But it is important to note how one's happiness is sustained through our ongoing actions, and if we continue to perform such actions, we perform more and more actions over time. As they analyzed the data from their studies and compared it to the generous actions in everyday life, they discovered that happiness is a series of actions that happen in a circular manner. In fact, it works in an upward spiral effect, which is to say, the more actions you perform for good, the more happiness you have, and the more you continue to perform more actions over time and increase their frequency and intensity.

What was also very interesting about their study that is worth noting is that the actions of generosity and doing good needed to be sustained over time and not just be episodic. The act of giving and supporting continually is essential for the individual to feel that ongoing warm glow and happiness effect. Therefore, as social movement builders, it is important to continue this activity so as to maintain that internal happiness.

Lastly, as we look at the types of people we help and interact with, there is no surprise that most of the individuals will likely help family members and those closest to us. But the hardest step is to help the unknown—the person with little or no connection to the one providing support. This is a step that we take when we perform more actions and also start to be exposed more to the needs of others. Helping the person we don't know can have an immense impact on the happiness of the individual supporter. This is key in social movement building because, for the most part, the movement amasses people who may not be intimately affected, yet are yearning to make a difference.

IMPLICATIONS FOR SOCIAL MOVEMENTS

From these studies, we can see that happiness is linked to our empathetic side to help one another. There are good effects one receives when supporting a social movement or an act for good. The most important thing to note, though, is the need to perform ongoing actions rather than just

one. Social movements need to incorporate ongoing acts of good to maintain the level of interest and internalized happiness that one can obtain.
It is the act of doing good continually that needs to be sustained because
the benefits can affect both the movement and the person immensely.
Social movement builders have an opportunity to spark engagement
because of our empathy and altruism. The true test is whether a true
movement is built out of these small and personalized actions for
long-term change.

Chapter 2 Creating a Movement ... Through Empathy

James Coan
Professor, University of Virginia

When we think about why people get involved in social movements, it's hard to ignore the empathy that we have for the inequalities and challenges we see and feel when we see others suffering. It goes back to the makeup and emotional behaviors of the brain. One individual who has been at the forefront of this work has been Professor James (Jim) Coan of the University of Virginia.

Jim began his work in the early nineties watching how couples and individuals have conflict with each other. He observed conversations, tones, and discussions between individuals who were at odds with one another because of marital or partnership disputes. What was amazing about the research Jim was a part of was coming to see how couples who fight learn how to handle conflict with each other well and those who do not. He realized all couples would fight, but it was the unspoken emotional support provided to each other that helped bring the couples through their challenges and disputes. He realized that everyone has negative interactions, but those who are good at defusing the situations are those who stick together and eventually increase their happiness. For the most part, he saw these individuals who were closely tied to each other interact in unexpressive ways. Not that these individuals would immediately say "Oh, my spouse is very upset," they would just act to make it better. For the most part, the individual didn't even realize that he or she was doing anything to defuse the situation. It became just part of who they were.

The bond that these individuals had with one another really meant so much not just to the individual but to the both of them to cope, handle, and celebrate life's challenges and successes. Jim also noticed this years later when he was doing psychotherapy work with a World War II veteran who could not endure any treatment for post-traumatic stress disorder without his wife there holding his hand. Unless his wife was holding his hand, clasping it in a way to show love and affection, this individual would not talk or undergo any treatment. The bond he had with his wife helped him overcome the traumas he had to deal with.

It was from this experience that Jim began to test a theory about holding hands with others. He found that if someone was holding hands with another, preferably with a spouse, the individual could endure pain and challenges more than if he or she wasn't. The brain, throughout the experiments, would use the interaction and bonding moment as a salve for the pain and suffering.

His theory on hand-holding is based on the ecology of the human. Jim describes how if you are a salamander, your brain seeks a cool, damp, dark space under a rock to find comfort. If you can't find such a place, the brain has a distressed reaction and tries to find one. The brain tells that salamander to search for a place that is comfortable. Just like the salamander, a human holding hands with another person can be comfortable. It is a natural environment to be in. It is built within the human brain and ethos of the individual to be empathic and supportive through bonds and relationships.

This was further explored in a famous study that involved backpacks. In the study, the researchers brought individuals to an area where they were asked to walk a certain distance uphill. These individuals perceived the hills to be steep but not too difficult to climb. But when the individuals were wearing heavy backpacks, the hills seemed to be much steeper. It was perceived to be an incredibly daunting task for the individuals to overcome. Jim explains that the brain is designed to play perceptual tricks to motivate the individual to take one behavioral course over another. In essence, at times we don't really perceive the world as it really is.

In the backpack study, the researchers added a new component and twist to test the brain's ability to react differently. After the individual was given a heavy backpack, he or she was standing next to his or her best friend. When the individual was standing next to his or her best friend, the backpack effect, or challenging perception, started to diminish. The individuals started to see the hills as less challenging. The deduction from the research is that the individual wearing the backpack saw the other individual as a valuable resource. The bond and support between them was comforting and allowed each individual to overcome the perception that overwhelmed them.

This leads to Jim's further studies around friends and other intimates. He found that when your friend is under the threat of shock, pain, or other challenge, your brain responds almost exactly as if you are under the same threat of shock, pain, or challenge as your friend is. But when a stranger is under the threat of shock, your brain still responds, you still know things about that person's experience, but you don't respond as if it's you. You don't respond as if you are under the same threat. You only respond accordingly when the threat is to your friends or family. This further suggests that as we develop a relationship with somebody else, we start to identify with him or her. We start to become more like each other.

This brings us to the relationship process that can aid in our understanding of empathy. According to Jim, the process of developing a relationship is the process of coming to understand that someone else understands me. He or she strongly believes my point of view and the point of view of everyone else involved with me. Then the individual starts to respond to this other person's situation as if it's his or her own situation. This brings us to the empathy side of the human, that is exhibited within the relationships of social good and cause interest. Essentially, an individual has empathy within him- or herself because individuals want to act on another's behalf when he or she feels what the sufferer feels and they want to be a social support mechanism, similar to the holding-hands experiment.

Jim believes that if we assume another person's experience is very much like ours and that they're suffering, we suffer on their behalf. That is the empathetic response we often see. But if we're the ones suffering and the person we love and trust and empathize with is actually not, we also, it turns out, empathize with their lack of suffering and our own suffering decreases. He states that the ability to care about someone else uses the same machinery as the ability to know that someone else is caring about us.

In my discussion with Jim, I asked about why the individual responds and reacts to social movements, especially when it comes to the use of activism online such as through Twitter, Facebook, or other forms of social networking. His ideas about this go beyond the current thinking by some in the field. We have all heard about Millennials doing things because of their passion and interests, leading to larger levels of engagement. But the initial reaction and support in an online social media network is based on the brain acting economically.

Jim explained that the brain likes to work as little as possible. Brains are like a budgeting executive trying to maintain a balance between expending time and energy to get the best possible outcome. The brain is essentially an economic machine looking for the easiest and most efficient route to achieve a desired outcome. At some times the brain will preserve some resources to use them at a later date when the return will be much greater. So in an era of social activism online, it is not unreasonable to see individuals participating in campaigns without going in the field or getting their hands dirty because the brain says to the individual, the need to help others and bring those feelings of empathy and compassion can happen when you post or share something that provides a sympathetic feeling back to the individual. In essence, the brain sees it as a unique opportunity to get some satisfaction without necessarily performing any physical engagement for the cause. "If you can be activists while sitting in your chair, it's going to take off because it's super easy for the brain to be a part of," he said.

Jim's theories of social engagement with causes help explain the behavior that is often exhibited. The real challenge for some will be taking that built-in mechanism of support for others and building stronger relationships that will lead the enthusiast to the self-organizing activist level and beyond.

Chapter 3 From Belonging to Owning a Movement

I do not belong to a movement, I believe in the movement and am the movement. I am not a donor, volunteer, or supporter. I am a believer in the movement and I like to share that belief with my friends.

—Interview, cause activist

We started the Millennial Impact Project, a comprehensive research study that started in 2009 on how the Millennial generation engages with causes, with the purpose of helping institutions connect and involve this generation of cause enthusiasts. We knew we had a group of individuals wanting to get involved in causes because of their exposure to the cause world in school and family, but for some reason that activation wasn't happening how it historically has. Moreover, we saw institutions that were in existence for more than 50 years struggling to develop relationships with Millennials even though this interest in causes existed. We therefore knew that the studies were necessary to help transform the thinking and approach of why a Millennial will get involved in a cause. Our approach was never to compare Millennials to the Baby Boomers or the Greatest Generation, which so many want to know at times. Rather, the goal was to talk in isolation about a generation that is ready and willing to get involved in causes and to help bridge the gap through research and understanding.

Because of the project and my role as the lead researcher, I am often asked to meet with organizations to discuss their interest in working with us about Millennial engagement. This is part of the job I really enjoy, getting the chance to connect directly with those who are consistently in the field seeking to build a stronger relationship with their constituents. But there is something that I have noticed over time, especially in recent days, that has us challenging the overall approach to giving and serving: Causes really want to raise money and gain the attention of every individual they can. For selfish reasons, the cause is seeking a "silver bullet" to gain a competitive advantage over others in the hope that their cause will win the fundraising gold mine.

As organizations reach out, I like to ask some questions during our time together to get at the real intent of the interest in working with us. After 10 to 15 minutes of the organization's leaders explaining what has been happening, that is, the decline in membership, a community of people who aren't doing anything, a stagnant donor base, or the struggles in creating a message that will get a higher response, it comes out that the real reason for the call was to fix their programs, which have been in decline for years. They hope we will, through our research, observations, and experience, drive enormous traffic to their site, skyrocket actions from individuals such as Millennials, and majorly increase incoming donations.

What is also apparent throughout the conversation is that the organization's *ideologies* are misaligned. The concept of organizing, fundraising, and movement building is focused on an individual "belonging" to a cause. It sounds funny, but it's true. If you listen to the individuals who lead the outreach efforts for the cause, they will use phrases such as the following:

"Our donors"
"Our sponsors"
"Our group does not do that"
"Our ambassadors do this for us"
"We have volunteers who do this for us"
"Our community of people"

During the conversation, this language and phrasing seeps into the regular discourse we have and makes me wonder, what do the people who are their donors, sponsors, and ambassadors feel about being or belonging to that organization?

But that isn't how today's causes build movements. The movement isn't owned by the entity but rather the people of the movement itself. This goes to the realities of today's constituent engagement theory and how people are now perceived in today's causes as activists, supporters, and donors who are crucial to the makeup of a successful movement. In the research that we have conducted, it is apparent that younger demographics view themselves as *of* a cause and not *for* a cause. They don't belong to a cause but rather believe in the work of the cause and therefore act as they do because of that belief, not because they joined it or belonged officially at some point.

This shift is a cultural one in how we view people in today's social movements for good. It is a shift that leaders and social movement builders need to grasp so they can be successful in harnessing the power of individuals for a common purpose. Let's examine five specific underpinnings and foundational concepts to social movement building that focus on how an entity, company, or cause should view people they want to engage.

EXPERIENCE OVER JOINING

If you run an association, a club, or a product forum, you may be wondering if you can create a movement that people need to join. The concept of joining and owning a relationship with an entity has been a historical model that causes and companies have used to gain two things: support and relationship building with members. Joining isn't a concept that social movement participants shy away from. It's about when it is introduced. Leading with joining means you have a high expectation. That expectation is that to be a part of the movement, we are only interested in those who are willing to participate at some certain level of money or time.

The joining approach is a belonging feature that discounts experiencing the brand and the cause issue. In other social movements, I don't need to join to show support for an issue. I can experience the social issue through peers and networks, learn through digital platforms about the plight of others, and tweet with fellow movement participants using a hashtag—all social good opportunities that have no barrier to entry.

In essence, the concept of becoming a member of something has been displaced by a different time within the individual's relationship with a cause. Being part of a social movement is about expressing one's belief in an issue. Joining is now an ultimate expression that should be used for those who want to experience an even deeper role with a cause and the issue they represent. But to experience a social issue and to build a movement, making it possible for the individual to talk, share, and express a belief, is a concept that some membership groups are not familiar with and will be challenged by those who want to move from a state of cause enthusiasm to social-movement engaging to cause supporter and eventually to donor and stakeholder.

ACTING WITHOUT PURPOSE

Did you ever watch someone act for a cause when he or she didn't truly care about the issue? This observation is something that I have witnessed, along with my team, many times over the years. Here is what happens when an individual participates in an act of altruism but the interest is truly lacking.

The individual is exposed to a cause or social issue message through external marketing, general awareness, or social influence. Social influence is a mechanism used to garner a reaction from an approach involving peers, friends, networks, leveraged opportunities (matches), or other behavior modeled by a population for a group to act. The intent of social influence is to help the individual understand why acting is imperative and to spark the empathic emotion one needs to make it possible to help another. This intent is at times overcome by an individual's personal interest to get his or her network to truly engage in a cause or issue. This helps to build the esteem, interest, and personal goals of the individual who represents the cause (usually informally).

Once the individual acts, not in personal interest but rather for alternative reasons, the individual internalizes alternative feelings outside of altruism. Typical responses to the requests made by others when the individual lacks true purpose and interest in a cause include the following:

"Sure, I guess so."
"It's for a good cause."
"I guess I could help out."
"I don't mind giving a few dollars."
"What's the harm in helping?"
"Why not? It's not a lot of money."
"I will get involved just this one time."

This observation is a reality for many. In looking at the acts of an individual in our recent study of Millennials, we discovered that only 40 percent acted in support of a cause for personal, philanthropic reasons. Therefore, 60 percent are acting out of support for ulterior motives of their network or social benefit.[1]

In looking at how and why individuals today perform the actions they do for causes, and repeat such actions within the same year and every year after, we notice that they do it because of purposeful reasons and not to merely participate. The social movements they engage with have hit on the purpose of current values and norms they express about social issues affecting them, the place, and people in their lives. In essence, the individual moves from episodic actions of cause engagement for others to purposeful engagement with a cause issue because of personal meaning. Therefore, acting without purpose occurs but does not add value to the social movement in the long-term and should be avoided.

TELLING IS LESS IMPORTANT THAN SELF-DIRECTING

In today's business culture and within communities across the country, the notion of decentralized environments is becoming the norm. Historically, companies used a top-down approach to employee activation. Whether the message and approach were for a product, service,

---

[1] 2015 Millennial Impact Report, Achieve.

employee-volunteering program, or corporate giving initiative, CEOs and the corner suite level would direct the company workforce to participate for the betterment of the company. This top-down approach enabled CEOs to direct the workforce without asking questions, seek input, or be challenged on initiatives. Although action may occur, the individual internalizes the action as a response to a request, rather than for personal interests.

Rather than telling someone to be involved in a social movement, we see that as another expression of one's interest in a cause, one can discover the issue and self-direct their involvement. Social movements create an opportunity for one to participate *with* the group rather than *for* the group. This participation also gives a social movement activist the chance to develop his or her own participation track with the issue. The cause or company becomes a beneficiary of the individual and their journey to self-direct his or her ideas and support for a cause rather than telling the supporter what to do and how to do it. In essence, the person's self-directed behavior is more important than the response of their actions, although necessary in order to maintain the social movement.

Self-directed approaches allow the individual to express interest, make the cause his or her own, and create a personalized journey of interests for the social issue. These benefits enable the community to spread organically, authentically, and with purpose based on the individual taking ownership of the relationship with the issue. Social movements today need self-directed models to ensure that the individual doesn't join but self-actualizes the movements as part of the individual's personality and purpose. This helps to maintain interest and passion in the cause and issue over time.

INCLUSIVITY BEATS VIP

One of the best sayings in philanthropy today is that performing the act of giving and serving is one of the best levelers in society. In essence, the act of helping another isn't an exclusive experience to those with money and resources. Social movements are an inclusive opportunity. If the social issue speaks to the purpose and interests of the individual, one can perform an act in support without having a minimal level of assets or experience.

In the social movements we have observed and also the organizations behind them, we notice that these institutions treat all individuals equally. Their individual donors receive similar benefits as major donors. Key volunteers receive similar benefits like episodic volunteers do. Personalization, communication, and messages that speak to the value the individual brings to the collective are often the case in marketing and promotional materials. Individuals also receive perceived access to the benefits of being associated with the social issue. These include, but are not limited to, transparency reports about the impact of money and people on the issue, opportunities to attend events and programming, and opportunities to meet and discuss their interests with the staff and leadership of the cause. All of these help bring the individual closer to the people who oversee the movement and the network of people who make the social movement for good possible.

Exclusive opportunities afforded to a population of social movement participants versus others is a detractor to the movement itself. The social movement requires individuals who can feel like their participation makes a difference that an organization is accepting, is thankful, and excited to receive. The latter is vital to the success of encouraging an individual to spread the social movement to his or her network. If the donors believe the organization values their contributions, and they receive benefits for being a supporter, they will tell their friends and colleagues about that experience, resulting in the movement growing in depth and breadth.

SELF-REALIZING IS POWERFUL

It is one thing to talk about social issues and the problems facing others. It is another to realize it through expression and experience. Organizations today have at their disposal the tools and approaches to help an individual experience the issues they want to address. From film to social media, we can become closer and closer to the realities of the change necessary to solve social problems. The media has created an environment in which their reporting and timeliness of the story can greatly influence our ability to join a social movement.

For example, if you look at natural disaster fundraising and movement building, you will notice that the vast majority of support comes within the first couple of weeks of the disaster. The media, on the ground citizen storytellers and documentarians, and individuals sharing the images of the people hurt and the suffering they endured, fuels this response. The individual in receipt of such messages responds naturally to the suffering and images due to the empathic impulse and love they have for helping others.

The experience of viewing images and other media helps the individual realize the challenges others are enduring. This goes beyond simple words—letting the images and narratives of personal stories translate into the major message for the public to react to.

Social movements and causes need to help the individual understand the issues they are trying to support. This means that the public must understand the individual affected, the challenge he or she is undertaking, and that there are others out there who share the beliefs those individuals do about the issue. Narratives of social movements must go beyond aspirational-type language and be realistic to the issues at hand, and how their involvement can make a difference. It is also important that the organization follows up with the individual's action to ensure it understands how such participation was realized and that change has occurred. Without the opportunities to self-realize the social issue, the attachment is short-lived and moves to a more distant view of ever changing or getting better.

BELIEVING IN IS BETTER THAN BELONGING TO

In the end, social movements are about believing in an issue rather than belonging to one. Today's social activists, supporters, and donors are looking for a cause to be a part of what they believe in. The relationship with the entity is less important than the resonance to and being of an issue. This is supported through the research we have conducted on Millennial generation activists, donors, and volunteers. Their interest in the institution itself is less than with the issue the institution represents.[2]

In addition to believing in the cause, the individual must believe in the social movement builder and the entity driving the movement itself. The social movement builder is an influential storyteller and a representative of the values and beliefs of the movement. They embody the

---

[2]2013, Millennial Impact Report, Achieve.

movement and personalize the story of the movement for the public to react to. The social movement builder, though, is not the movement itself. The movement is about the people affected by the social issue. The leader and organizer help the people share, experience, and express themselves through the movement. This concept of being *of* the movement rather than being the movement itself will determine the extent of the movement's ability to garner public attention.

In translation, this means that the general public needs a movement to believe in: A social issue that will affect the community they interact with, the people in their network, and the values they believe in. Believing in a cause and an issue builds the sustaining power of the movement.

Movements are not about one individual belonging, but rather a group of people believing in a common purpose. Organizations need to realize this important characteristic of social movements for it to be successful. Once the organization tries to influence or exert its personal interests, the movement will retaliate and potentially disband. It is no longer about common purpose but the interests of how the entity will gain from its association and management of the movement.

HEADLINE: ALS ASSOCIATION WITHDRAWS CONTROVERSIAL APPLICATIONS TO TRADEMARK "ICE BUCKET CHALLENGE"

Abby Ohlheiser, *Washington Post*, August 30, 2014[3]

With controversy swirling, the ALS Association announced that it would withdraw its applications to trademark the phrases "ice bucket challenge" and "ALS ice bucket challenge."

One trademark attorney calls the effort "shameful."

Two trademark applications, filed last week, claim that the ALS Association owns the phrases for the purposes of charitable giving. Both applications are available for public viewing on the U.S. Patent and Trademark Office website, here and here.

Trademark attorney Erik Pelton spotted the applications Wednesday. "I was upset," he told *The Post*. "Similar to the reaction I had last year when

(continued)

---

[3] www.washingtonpost.com/news/post-nation/wp/2014/08/28/can-the-als-association-trademark-the-ice-bucket-challenge-its-going-to-try/.

(continued)

I saw the applications for "Boston Strong." The latter phrase was a popular rallying cry in the wake of the Boston Marathon bombings.

While Pelton believes that the "ice bucket challenge" trademark applications will probably be rejected, the applications themselves were enough for the Virginia-based attorney to draw attention to them on his blog. "The reasons in general one seeks to protect a trademark is to prevent others from using it," Pelton said in an interview Thursday. "I find this to be shameful, because I hope that they would never consider … preventing some other charity from using the phrase."

In his blog post about the application, Pelton writes that he's "not sure they can claim real ownership" of the phrases in question, pointing out that "many others have taken the challenge in the name of (and/or contributed to) other charities." In the interview, he added: "It's been great to raise awareness and money."

THE IMPORTANCE FOR SOCIAL MOVEMENTS

Understanding how people interact with causes, products, and entities is important to move enthusiasm and interest to action. Belonging is not as important as believing in the purpose and values of the social movement. Social movement builders and the organizations they oversee must ensure the principles of purpose, authenticity, and self-realization are present. Without these features, individuals cannot see the power of the movement in real time and their impact on the movement. This results in less sharing, less expressive measures that make social movements what they are—powerful communities of individuals who believe in a common purpose to make change happen.

Chapter 3   Creating a Movement … Finding Value in Every Individual

Adam Braun
Founder, Pencils of Promise

In 2008, Adam Braun, then an analyst for Bain and Company, founded the organization Pencils of Promise, with a mission to provide quality education to children in various countries to ensure they could excel and lead a prosperous life. The model he created focuses on the development of an educational environment in which locals provide quality education with a manager who deeply supports each child and nurtures their ability to learn and grow. This story of Adam is shared in his book, *The Promise of a Pencil*.

Although the full story of why he founded Pencils of Promise can be discovered in his book, the focus of our time together was on what he learned from creating the Pencils of Promise movement. This organization has grown to have more than 200 schools supporting more than 30,000 students. After a careful review of the Pencils of Promise model and in talking with Adam, it was clear that the organization was built on the power of the individual to affect change and believe in the concept of education Adam was able to convey. Adam's core work around movement building also yielded its most success when he was able to help the individual donor and activist in the circle of the organization understand the power of their action. All of this can be found in the excerpts and concepts that follow.

MOVEMENT MESSAGE

From the beginning, Adam was intentional about never using the word "I." There was always a purposeful use of the word "we" even in actions that he performed by himself and had to convey the importance of how the individual's past action yielded a milestone for a student they may have never met. He would use language such as "We went to this village"—to conceptually bring the activist into the circle of the solution.

Even as he continued to head to countries such as Laos or others, he felt it was important to build a sense of inclusiveness with the community of individuals who believe in the power of Pencils of Promise. Although individuals would ask about what's happening and comment on the impact he was personally having, he was quick to correct and say, "No, no, no, it's not something that *I* did or that *you* did. It's something that *we* did. So don't say *you* to me. You're part of this as well. This is your organization." At one point, Braun even ordered business cards that labeled the individual's role in making a difference for a Pencil of Promise student. He would distribute these and later discovered how much this small act of ownership meant so much to those who received them.

In the early days of the organization's development, Adam was very intentional on using the word *movement*. He believed strongly that if others felt the momentum, the desire, and excitement of others as part of the organization, so many would believe that they could make a difference with others. Use of the word showed up on early marketing materials and to this day, the word *movement* is still used to convey the power of individual activists and supporters.

ALL ASSETS AS EQUALS

Adam believed that to be part of a movement, you have to be willing and able to support the effort through many different means. The organization built a widget to allow any individual to donate in three different ways: donate your time, donate your money, or you could donate your voice. Individuals who donated their voice could post a status about Pencils of Promise.

> And so I would talk to people all the time—people who did not have jobs and would say things like, "Look, I don't have any money. How can I help you?" And I would say, "Well, you can donate your status or donate your voice or you know there are a lot of different ways in which you can add value to the movement."

THE NEED TO SHOW

Ninety-nine percent of the people who interact with Pencils of Promise will never actually see their work in person. From the beginning, Adam believed in the need for a powerful website that used imagery and video to help convey the needs of the students in the countries where they were active. The experience of the website was imperative for those not about to go on trips with Adam's team. For the most part, he felt that website utility and user experience was missing in the storytelling process of the organization to connect donor and beneficiary. Investments in technology helped bring the organization's work closer to the activists. But Adam was still at the forefront of all design decisions—making comments, directing graphic designers and his team with an acute eye toward perfection—all in the spirit of showing the power of the movement. They have used technology solutions such as GPS to allow website users to track progress and see firsthand the power of the work on the ground, and Silverlight to use a camera and take photos inside and have an immersive 3D experience—all bringing the user closer and closer to the need.

FINDING COMFORT WITH THE ASK

Adam is a self-proclaimed "shy guy" when it comes to asking, never was completely comfortable with asking for money.

> I just, I didn't like viewing the work from a sales perspective. I like, you know, I'm an on the ground person. I'm a program person. I wanted to go be in these communities, work with these communities. Sure, if people wanted to support it, great, but I wasn't going to put my beliefs on them.

But this position would eventually change over time as he started to realize that people like to be asked to help and offer support. As he continued to build the organization and was able to show how they made a difference, he realized that he was doing them a service to show and guide them how to do more through an "ask" for support. He viewed it as a way to bring "value into their lives by enabling them to use their resources to improve the life of somebody else."

FINDING A NEW ROLE WITH COMPANIES

In 2010 and 2013, Adam deployed a strategy that would capitalize on partnerships with companies. The partnerships included sponsorship cause marketing campaigns and other external public relations–type programs that would help the organization expand its reach and potential awareness with general audiences. Although successful, this strategy was a little removed from their approach with individuals—creating strong individual relationships with constituents to build the movement.

In 2013, they shifted focus with companies by moving beyond the traditional cause relationships seen with other national organizations to their workforce. Getting back to their original strategy of people engagement, the organization has now developed stronger partnerships with companies that allow them to educate, inspire, and build momentum internally through individual employee participation with Pencils of Promise.

Campaigns have now been created that target employees raising support as personal fundraisers and developing internal incentives and competitions for the employees to participate at higher levels. Leadership and supervisors were more active through this approach, which centered less on the external corporate public relations angle and more on helping the individual move from a passive voice in cause marketing campaigns to being a much more active participant.

Today the organization is working with companies to incorporate the Pencils of Promise experience even into the benchmarks of the company as an opportunity. For example, some company partners now offer trips with Pencils of Promise if goals are met. The message has moved partially away from just a personal benefit to helping others. Messages such as "if you hit your sales marks, you're going to get a $2,000 bonus" is being replaced with "if you hit your sales marks, you're going to win an opportunity to go into the field with Pencils of Promise to see this school that you helped create by virtue of your performance in the company."

ENGAGEMENT MEANS SOMETHING DIFFERENT TO EVERYONE

To Adam and the Pencils of Promise team, they view engagement with the organization as a personal thing. The individual is the one who defines that relationship with the organization and moves into an ambassadorial role in some way on his or her own terms. Once they feel like they "own" the organization, asking to help or act is less daunting because they have internalized the concept of Pencils of Promise as their cause.

Pencils of Promise has varying levels of these types of ambassadors. Some leaders are engaged by being on the advisory board, which is a three-year financial commitment. Some executives are on the board of directors, which is the fiduciary oversight, governance, and support mechanism for the staff leadership. There are others who are engaged by reading Adam's book, or buying a T-shirt, and showing their pride and enthusiasm with their network. Whatever the level, Pencils of Promise and Adam believe strongly that there is value the person brings to the table, and it is their role to honor and support that value.

SOCIAL MEDIA AND SOCIAL CAUSE INVOLVEMENT

Adam and his team realize the potential of social media and the advances in social giving and technology to help any individual advocate and raise support for a favored cause. In the past, it was more difficult to organize with friends and networks—the sharing component of the message was much more difficult than ever before. We now continue to see new technologies that build and advance the concept of social cause engagement. When I had a chance to visit with Adam, he commented that in the past 24 hours, an individual launched a campaign and was on the verge of surpassing $100,000 in support for Pencils of Promise—something unheard of 10 years ago. Adam points out the immense power an individual can have today in a comment he made to me.

> I think the power of individuals creating an army of torchbearers by giving them the tools and technology to advocate is an unreal opportunity. Essentially, you want individuals to recognize their personal capacity to create change through your organization. And then to collectively recognize the sum of those parts being greater than the individual pieces is a remarkable feat and feeling we owe to the power of technology.

THE FUTURE IS SMALL GROUPS

Adam believes the next phase of social engagement is small groups. He has seen the power of technology combined with resources for individuals help bolster the small group impact model. This model is based on individuals creating their own experiences, opportunities, learning environments, and marketing for and on behalf of a cause they care about. Small cohorts and teams will drive the necessary work causes will be doing in the future, and thus an individual and group strategy will be necessary.

He sees this taking more hold because schools and companies have expanded their efforts to bring people together for a common purpose and goal. Group learning styles, teams, departments, and growth in decentralized cultures have led to a point of cause engagement at the grassroots individual and group level. Adam recognizes that some critics will view this as an online strategy only, but in reality it will also be offline. He views this engagement and all such engagements for causes having two polarizing spectrums—complete online engagement and complete offline engagement. Neither is more correct than the other, but it is a spectrum of involvement that organizations will need to be prepared to support.

REFLECTION

Over the years, I have had an opportunity to interact with Adam Braun and some of his team. We have monitored campaigns they have created, monthly giving programs, digital, and in-person engagement. Some may have looked at the Adam Braun story of founding Pencils of Promise as a similar story to others in the field of international cause development.

What I find fascinating about his work is the personal value he places on people. Forget the great website he creates or the beautifully designed pieces for the campaigns that have energized so many. The true power is the core belief that all people matter in the Pencils of Promise equation. This is a profound and underlying theme that seems so simple but yet rarely and authentically replicated by other movement builders.

Adam Braun will be successful in many things going forward, whether he is at Pencils of Promise or leading the biggest company in the world. What will truly matter is his ability to bring people with him and for what he champions. The secret lies in the belief that anyone is of the movement, for the movement, and a part of the movement. That mentality is something that makes him stand out above the rest and makes the cause he is working on a movement truly worth noting.

Chapter 4 Creating a Message to Believe In

It was February 3, 2013, and I was at a friend's house watching the Super Bowl. The game was a close one between the Baltimore Ravens and the San Francisco 49ers. This was appropriately titled the Harbaugh Bowl because the coaches of each opposing team were brothers Jim Harbaugh of the 49ers and John Harbaugh of the Ravens.

For some, the game was just a time to get together and visit with friends while watching one of the biggest sporting events of the year. In fact, the Super Bowl in 2013 attracted more than 160 million viewers. This was a record in the number of viewers to any Super Bowl.

For others, it was a time to get together to watch some great commercials. Consumer brands spent that year an average of $4 million for a 30-second commercial to be played during the game. With so many people watching, big brands couldn't pass up the opportunity to show the latest concepts, ideas, and creative energies to engage the American public with their products and services.

I had just gone downstairs during a commercial break at my friend's house to see his latest project—he was remodeling his basement and was quite proud of the progress so far. After coming back upstairs, I sat next to my wife, Bis, and she was talking with one of her friends about how great the commercial was. She was very moved by what she heard. It was very telling of how we view farmers.

Then she looked at me and said, "Derrick, aren't you doing work with FFA (Future Farmers of America)?" I said, "Yes, but why?" "Because you have to see the commercial we just saw." Her next words echoed the sentiment of everyone else in the room. "I don't have any personal connections to farming, but it was pretty incredible."

Well, I had to see what I missed. So I quickly went to my phone and then tracked down the video on YouTube. The commercial started with an image of a field and a cow. In the blue sky, in an older typewriter-style typeface, the words "Paul Harvey" showed up. Paul Harvey was a conservative radio broadcaster for ABC Radio Networks. Each weekday, his show *News and Comment* provided listeners in the morning and midday the opportunity to hear the latest news and commentary from his point of view. In addition to this show, Harvey had a segment and series called *The Rest of the Story*. This program highlighted facts and information that the general public was not yet aware of. The main story line throughout the piece would be followed by a big reveal of a famous issue, concept, or person. At the height of his popularity, more than 24 million people every week heard his voice on more than 1,200 radio stations and 400 Armed Forces Network stations, and read his commentary in 300 newspapers.

In 1978, at the Future Farmers of America (FFA) annual convention meeting, Paul Harvey delivered the keynote address. FFA focuses on students growing their leadership skills, talents, and experiences in agriculture to groom the next farmer, food innovator, and agricultural stakeholder. FFA has more than 600,000 members in the United States, Puerto Rico, and the U.S. Virgin Islands.

The commercial went on to recite Harvey's speech in his own words with a backdrop of images. The images consisted of farmers in the field, in American towns, and with their families. Close-ups of farmers and their proud ancestry, their hands, and the actions they take every day were used to help the public understand the work of a farmer. The images made a very humanistic connection between the viewer and the farmer they had never met. This was done while tastefully adding in the Dodge Truck in such images where appropriate—not as the focal point but as a part of the story.

The most impactful component of the commercial was Harvey's message about farmers. The following is an excerpt from his speech at the FFA convention in 1978 and was used in the 2013 Super Bowl commercial.

> And on the eighth day, God looked down on his planned paradise and said, "I need a caretaker." So God made a farmer.

> God said, "I need somebody willing to get up before dawn, milk cows, work all day in the field, milk cows again, eat supper, then go to town and stay past midnight at a meeting of the school board." So God made a farmer.

> God said, "I need somebody willing to sit up all night with a newborn colt and watch it die, then dry his eyes and say, maybe next year. I need somebody who can shape an ax handle from a persimmon sprout, shoe a horse with a hunk of car tire, who can make a harness out of haywire, feedsacks, and shoe scraps. Who, planting time and harvest season will finish his 40-hour week by Tuesday noon and then, paining from tractor back, put in another 72 hours." So God made a farmer.

> God said, "I need somebody strong enough to clear trees and heave bales, yet gentle enough to yean lambs and wean pigs and tend the pink-comb pullets, who will stop his mower for an hour to splint the leg of a meadowlark." So God made a farmer.

> It had to be somebody who'd plow deep and straight and not cut corners. Somebody to seed, weed, feed, breed, and rake, and disk, and plow, and plant, and tie the fleece and strain the milk. Somebody who'd bale a family together with the soft, strong bonds of sharing, who would laugh, and then sigh and then reply with smiling eyes when his son says that he wants to spend his life doing what Dad does. So God made a farmer.[1]

The commercial ends with a message that reads "To the farmer in all of us." It was a moving moment for the viewer to see. The message grabbed our attention at a time, during the Super Bowl, when so many other messages and commercials were trying to capture any moment of interest we may have.

---

[1] https://www.youtube.com/watch?v=AMpZ0TGjbWE.

The commercial was created for the benefit of the FFA Foundation and organization. Chrysler, the parent company of the Dodge brand, committed $100,000 for every 100,000 people who watched the video up to a $1 million. This was accomplished in less than five days. Today the video has more than 18 million views on YouTube. The message was sent and received loud and clear.

WHY A MESSAGE?

Movements are built by and for the people.

The people generate the movement, spread the rallying cry of the message, and depend on one another to meet the collective's goals in addressing the social issue at hand. The people, though, are bound by a common vision and a common narrative—to change the course of an issue that has affected so many people.

But how is this possible?

How can an individual turn his or her attention from the general issues present in so many communities to the importance of one issue affecting a group of people they may have never met before? Or take a stand for a concept that may never even affect them personally?

It comes down to the message and a story. A story based on a vision for change for people or communities that need it most.

ELEVATING THE PERSON IN THE CONTEXT OF THE CROWD

At the disposal of any individual today is the power of technology to do good. Now, more than ever, someone can create his or her own movement, build support for his or her interests and causes, and bring others in through their social networks. In essence, today's technology has democratized the activism more than ever before.

What does this mean for today's ability to start a new movement? The individual is now more powerful in the social movements of today than ever before.

Today's individuals can use simple and free technology tools to amplify a message while also gathering more movement momentum through the shared networks of like-minded activists.

What that means for today is a powerful environment for success. In fact, as we examine the movements of today, we find that the founders and movement builders began with a heavy focus on the individual and increasing their value in the movement.

This value was created through several key strategies that the movement founders made clear from the beginning was a major focus of their efforts and have remained constant since the organizations and movements they created began.

YOU

The core message in the movements of today centralize every message on the power of the word YOU. "You are the individual who can make helping another person possible." From the beginning, the message has maintained a constant activist central position to elevate the importance of the individual in the movement as part of the solution. This central language helps to constantly position the individual as part of a "warm glow" effect in which, with their support, the outcome is even more within reach and the individual positioned in the narrative is more likely to be affected. The marketing message never breaks form with the individual central opportunity. The message also maintains a constant individual focus with positioning as opportunistic in light of the power the individual can bring to the table now and in the future. The use of "we" is only used to represent the collective of the group and not the organization. This is very apparent in most messages that come from the group to the group in reference to accomplishment and achievement with public goals. This is further reiterated in imagery when groups of fellow movement participants are positioned as an opportunity to make change rather than take leadership of the organization. Leadership is positioned second in messages to give higher ranking to the concept and solution the movement is trying to accomplish.

CONCEIVABLE OUTCOME

In the messaging presented in today's movements we see a common benchmark established that is represented as a conceivable outcome. The message presented to the individual activist is positioned in a way that makes the individual feel success is near and very achievable. Through small actions and achievable steps taken by the individual, the collective is much closer than ever before. The conceivable outcome is usually presented in the form of small actions of sharing, getting others to support the individual's campaign during a time in his or her life like a birthday or wedding. The conceivable outcome doesn't tackle the issue per se in broad terms such as: if you sign this petition, world hunger will end tomorrow—but rather in terms of incremental change. If you sign this today, your power, with the combined power of other signatures, will get this small act passed and placed on the docket. That is all we need to be successful this week. Each act provides a conceivable action that makes getting on board with the cause and makes the issue less daunting and more personally rewarding. This almost takes a "gameification" approach to activism that inspires the individual to move and achieve conceivable outcomes rather than wait to accomplish global challenges that may or may not be plausible.

PARTICIPATORY LANGUAGE

Are you in? This was a phrase used by the Girl Effect in a campaign to make girls impossible to ignore. This phrase alone—Are You In?— invokes a message of participation that gains momentum in the movement. Participatory language implying a concept of "We are waiting for you and your powerful network to join others" with "This is the time we need you now more than ever," yields a strong emotional response of urgency and participation one cannot ignore. Participatory language sets the stage for the individual to feel compelled to act rather than wait for an additional learning opportunity or exposure point by the organization in the future. Participatory language has also yielded the greatest effect when coupled with personalization in the approach and message in an effort to make the individual concept of YOU the most powerful it can be. Participatory language is also combined with imagery at times to help the individual see the power of the collective. This is commonly done with historical campaigns such as PBS and others in which average people were present to voice their participation and support. This is true today through the power of social networks and media to publicly display the support offered for the movement.

ONE PERSON AFFECTED

The story of the movement is focused on the one individual affected. The individual, because of the circumstance, needs an army of people to help overcome a challenge and to build upon what is possible when people unite for a common purpose. Individuals begin to become the face of the issue at hand—the issue that the movement participants are eager to fight for. The individual story of challenges through media, imagery, and in social networks inspires others to drive for interest in support of the movement itself. Movements created tend to focus on two types of individuals: those who can relate to the movement participants and those who cannot.

The individual's story tends to bring to light how relatable the movement is for those who participate. The individual represents someone the movement participant can see next door, run into at the grocery store, and care for if needed because the circumstance is relatable to the individual. The story is built around the everyday challenges the individual faces, the issues he or she goes through that seem so common and minuscule to the movement participant. This drives the need and inspiration for someone outside the movement to join quickly because what happened to that victim of misfortune could at some point happen to him or her or someone close to him or her.

Another type of individual highlighted in movements is the complete opposite of the relatable individual who may represent the movement participant. In this case, the individual highlighted is someone representing the extreme of a situation. For example, this type of individual would be someone who lacks access to fresh water every day. This situation seems so implausible that it moves the individual immediately to an emotional state of deep concern and compassion. At times, the movement message creates a corollary connection to the individual. For example, this situation could be to compare the life of the participant to someone who needs help—resulting in drastic contrasts, such as a day in the life of someone with access to fresh water versus the struggle of someone who does not.

IMPACT IS IN THE EYE OF THE BEHOLDER

The movement successfully hooks the individual when he or she can see him- or herself as instrumental to the outcome—essentially leaving him- or herself with a higher level of personal impact than not having participated. The organizations that drive the movements create an important narrative of how the movement participant made a difference for someone. This message is used consistently throughout the post-activism fundraising phase of actions taken by participants. The message created would help the individual see periodically how their actions for the cause or issue in the movement had incremental change—and reinforces how without the individual's participation those helped would be less fortunate. Essentially, the movement marketer and fundraiser connects each action with an internal impact statement to reinforce the power of the individual in the movement.

WE ARE USING YOUR ASSETS NOW

Movements create incremental benchmarks and help movement participants understand at every step how their action, combined with others, is "moving the needle" on the issue. With the use of technology today, movement organizers have been able to create timed, personal, and automated communication through email and social media that drives the constant feedback mechanism to each movement participant. At each achievement of the movement, the individual is provided with a storyline that helps drive ongoing interest and participation to the next level. And at each level, the individual is able to see through images and witness through video how close the movement is to the accomplishment of what is next.

WITNESS THE BENEFICIARY

Movement organizers realize that not everyone will be able to be on the ground locally or will have the chance to meet a beneficiary firsthand, thus investments are made to bring the story of challenge and need to the movement participant. Through video and images, along with personal stories from the beneficiaries, individuals participating in the movement are able to feel like their actions can truly make a difference. Firsthand accounts of on-the-ground stories, interviews with those being helped, and images onsite help to bring the movement participant closer and closer to the action. We also tend to see movement creators establishing experiences for movement participants. Individuals will have the opportunity to gain access to the people or issue firsthand. All of this results in a degree of excitement that did not seem imaginable before.

IMPLICATIONS FOR SOCIAL MOVEMENTS

By examining some of today's movements, we see that movements are derived from a single narrative built around the person's ability to affect change. The narrative of any social movement depends on a narrative where people can read, witness, and feel other people being affected by issues. When an individual is able to make that personal connection to the challenge or the message of extreme pain, it transforms the individual into a state of concern and support that is so compelling to the success of the movement overall.

The narratives of movements may change from time to time, though, as more relevant events, policy changes, or resources are needed—but the core function of driving a common people-to-people message is maintained. The biggest driver to any movement will be the resounding interest of a populace interested in not just taking action online through social media but also driving change with further actions through the organization and not just for it. This is something that newer organizations have realized in creating today's movements. The work and message of the movement are not about the organization or for its success, but rather for the people affected and their success. The message of hope, change, and overcoming obstacles and challenges will supersede the message of the organization's board, the amount raised, and the number of people affected. People drive change with social movements with other people—a message that will never change even in today's multifaceted and connected world.

Chapter 4 Creating a Movement … With a Focus on Human-Centered Relevance

Azita Ardakani
Founder, Lovesocial

When the subject comes to messaging and movements today, it is hard to ignore the work that Azita Ardakani is doing for causes. As the head of Lovesocial, a communications agency based in New York City, she leads the team to build human-centered interactions for clients. Her clients happen to be organizations such as the Nature Conservancy and National Public Radio, all trying to garner and build an audience in an authentic way.

Azita sees social movements for good as a mechanism made up by a spontaneous group of people who are aligning on a common mission to make change. Their message is based on human-centered relevance, in which every voice matters to the force for good that the group is working toward.

When asking Azita about the concepts of human-centered relevance, she talked about a story of how people interact with an organization's mission and social purpose. She states that organizations, at their core, are composed of human interactions: the human interactions needed to solve a problem for a person in need, and the human interactions with donors and constituents to help them understand those challenges. All of these interactions are the threads that keep the organization together, from serving those who need help to helping those who can help understand the relevance of those who can't express their needs themselves. Organizations are at the heart of the individual interactions.

Azita also believes that people gravitate to causes when they can see how small acts can make notable differences in the outcome. By helping individuals realize that their actions can make an insurmountable change in an issue surmountable is important for social movement builders. This can be challenging when some social issues need take time to resolve or require a great amount of resources to accomplish. But as Azita puts it, this is something that must constantly be on the minds of the marketing and fundraising leadership of the organization and to work hard to simplify the action that can make a huge difference. This is the relevancy that is based on the human or individual becoming the hero in the narrative.

Azita believes successful social movements are based on the efforts of the people participating. Although some social movements have people participating at all levels of engagement, the successful movements have impassioned individuals who perform the acts of the movement because they believe deeply in the outcome, are personally tied to the outcome, and want to see the outcome be a reality. Azita believes that social movement builders need to be thoughtful about the type of people who should be participating in such movements for them to really gain traction. Some of the early adopters of a movement will naturally be some of the most engaged and loyal cause enthusiasts. Moving beyond this group of individuals as the movement grows, there should be a focus on bringing in more like-minded individuals. This representation goes beyond just taking action, but being a part of the movement itself.

In a discussion about social media and sharing, Azita mentions that today there is still a lack of understanding about social engagement. While some people will argue that social engagement with movements such as sharing and actions with peers on networks don't make change, it should be realized that to the individual participants, they are spending time—and that time is a representation of the value they place on an issue and topic. Social connectivity beyond just sharing an image is what drives us to tell others we care deeply about something. That social sharing is about human relationships, and those relevant relationships bring each of us closer to caring for one another's issues and its effects on one another.

Where social engagement has the highest impact can be through the images that break conversational barriers. People absorb images 50,000 times faster than text. Azita comments that the best part of today's social technology is our ability to share images that can deepen the connection to social issues and movements. Whether you are 8 or 85 years old, an image can have the same effect and thus unite a group of people who feel impassioned about an issue. The human-centered relevance that social sharing and images can have on people when we talk about the inequalities and challenges of our times can resonate with everyone.

Azita has worked with many different clients and social entrepreneurs. When talking about why some social movement builders fail, she is reminded of the individuals who start movements and assume that other people will care just because they do. This is a faulty assumption that usually affects the growth of any movement. She strongly believes that social movement builders always need to present the opportunity of the movement to others. With one nonprofit for every three hundred people in the United States, the nonprofit sector is a crowded area. The individual needs to present a meaningful story, and how that story reaches other individuals through the narrative.

In looking at the presentation that social movement builders need to make, she comments that someone with little to no context must be able to join the movement because of who they are. It is that clear and simple for the movement participant. By presenting an opportunity to act for the movement because it is relevant to them, it is who they are, and it is something their network is about, too, a unique opportunity is presented through which a movement can grow. This is the magic of social media today, where an individual can be a part of something larger than themselves at whatever level he or she wants with the people closest to them.

When thinking about social movement outcomes, Azita is quick to point out that the outcome itself is not always the goal of the movement. Success can be found in the form of international unity and coalition building that occurs because people came together. That alone is a measure of success. A step forward in a social issue is bringing people together who feel and have that natural connection because of who they are. Bringing that union of people to the next level through a series of actions for a particular outcome is a great and natural next step, but that first stage of coming together shouldn't be overlooked. Social movement builders must look at this step as a unique opportunity by itself as they create bonds between people everywhere.

I asked Azita about advice she would give to any social movement builder getting started. She said to remember that your one idea may be great, but it is sometimes better to join others and work together to make a movement happen. There are enough categories of causes and interests, so rather than start something new, join the tidal wave of someone else and help them build the movement they may not have been able to create. You may be the best person to help create that human-centered relevance they have been missing. Perhaps you can both see value in the way you want people to come together. That is the power of individuals working to create change through a social movement for good.

Chapter 5 Letting My Passion Be Heard through a Sign

SYMBOLISM AND THE SOCIAL MOVEMENT

One day, as I so often do as I wait for the others to board the plane, I began to check the day's social media mentions. My first stop is always Twitter, scrolling through the people, places, and organizations I have marked as my favorites in my feed.

I started to notice something. A few friends of mine recently changed their profile picture image to a symbol of three horizontal lines. At first I kind of let it go. I didn't see too much about it and thought to myself, there must be something they are championing—maybe in their local community or maybe it was something of an art contest and they were showing their support. Better yet, I convinced myself it was the latest sign for an event coming up.

No big deal.

I traveled overnight, stopping in Chicago on my way to New York. I arrived at the airport and was waiting for the next flight and as usual, I began to scroll through my social networks. This time I stopped to spend time looking over my Facebook page.

Something was different. It wasn't the same newsfeed that I have witnessed so many times before. This time, I noticed uniformity. Yes, every single profile started to look the same. The profiles of my friends, family, and organizations didn't reflect the variety of expression so eloquently (and at times a little distastefully) displayed in times before.

Everyone's profiles reflected the same symbol I had seen before. The symbol of what seemed now much more than a brand of an event. It was clear, this symbol had meaning and I was not part of it.

How could so many people in my feed share this common bond? Share this symbol of support for something? How could I not know of it?

Sitting in the airport, I thought, I will figure this out by listening to the news; CNN, of course, as in any airport. But I didn't hear a thing. No one mentioning a tragedy, per se. No mentions of a recent challenge or disaster.

What was going on? How was it possible that I was so in the dark?

Then it started to really get to me. How can everyone in my network participate in this? So I googled the symbol and discovered that this was no small thing.

The symbol was the representation of a movement. It was the Human Rights Campaign movement.

Ahh. Now it was starting to come to me. But why the three lines? What did it mean?

As I started to google and search for more meaning behind this viral symbol, I received a Facebook notification from my wife. It was the image of my oldest daughter getting ready for school—laughing and creating a funny face that just evoked cuteness.

Sure enough, my wife's profile image had changed to reflect the HRC symbol, too.

She called me to talk about the latest happenings of the morning, the usual push and pull of getting the kids ready and off to school.

I asked her, "What's the situation with your profile pic?"

"I believe gay and lesbian people should marry. I saw the symbol on my friend's Facebook page and couldn't help but change it because of how I feel about it."

I asked if she knew anything about the organization behind the symbol.

She said, "Not till I looked online."

This was common. My wife was like so many others willing to show their support to their network for the values they believed. Just three short days ago, my wife knew nothing about the organization. But the symbol meant something, and in less than 72 hours, she was now sharing with her closest people within her social network how she felt about it.

I was surprised because I didn't know what this would be like for the people who really didn't know her. Her Facebook community consisted of friends from high school and college. They are from all different areas of the world. And now she was telling them all.

I was proud.

Proud to be associated with her and proud that she was willing to show us what she believed in. And I was not alone. Many of her friends voiced their support as well, some she knew well and others she had not heard from or seen from in years.

In hearing my wife talk, there was a sense of pride. Pride in having that symbol in her profile pic. Pride in letting others know how she felt and not being afraid to let that symbol speak for her.

This is the power symbols can have on us. Symbols in social good movements represent a feeling, a value, and a belief. Symbols unite people who share a common purpose. And symbols create a sense of pride in the love we have for the people who need our support.

What is so impactful about a symbol is the recognition that words to explain the meaning aren't necessary. Individuals will stand proud behind carrying a symbol. And with social movements for good, symbols are necessary to let the passion and values unite a group of people.

SYMBOLISM IN TODAY'S SOCIAL MOVEMENTS

In looking at the latest trends when it comes to symbolism, we see that organizations are moving beyond simple brand and logo use and now to a concept of movement symbolism that reflects the story and narrative of the movement for the people. Historically, marketing may have looked at movements or campaigns from a singular brand motive. "How can we incorporate our brand into this message?" But today, we have seen brands move to the secondary position, away from the old adage that by influencing a person three times with the brand, he or she will remember it.

The movements of the past five years represent a new approach to marketing and message delivery—using a symbol to mark a concept or a piece of the issue rather than the entity itself. Take for example the latest movements outside the social good space. The following movements had no symbols associated with them but rather the use of words to reflect the notion of the movement or the issue needed to be overcome:

#bringbackourgirls
#standdontshoot
#handsup

In the social good space, the movement building represented needs an association mark to help it stand apart from the crowd of other issues. Different from social movements in general like the ones here that are about in-the-moment concepts that need to change or reflect a new public opinion, social movements are based on historical issues where under-represented individuals seek support and services. At any given moment, many causes can be vying for attention and never be able to achieve movement status. Those that do provide both the message and the rallying cry backed by the symbol.

WHY SYMBOLS?

It was August 28, 1963, and the steps of the National Mall in Washington, D.C. had more than 250,000 civil rights supporters. Crowds were packed from the Lincoln Memorial to the Washington Monument (see Figure 5.1). This speech was one of the most moving speeches in the history of the human race. The movement Dr. King represented was heard and felt as he brought forward the challenges of the civil rights movement as it was in the 1960s.

The speech was beautifully written to draw comparisons and bring in symbolism. From the beginning, Dr. King uses symbolic references to help those understand the issues of racial segregation and discrimination.

> Five score years ago, a great American, in whose symbolic shadow we stand today, signed the Emancipation Proclamation.

The symbolism of his speech, based on location and the story of civil rights, came through the rhetoric he amplified down the National Mall that day. From his references of the promissory note written by the "architects" of the Constitution and the Declaration of Independence to

FIGURE 5.1   Martin Luther King During the March on Washington, August 28, 1963[1]

the mentioning of the various locations throughout the country where freedom should ring, Dr. King created a vision that so many could conceptually understand and find compelling for anyone wanting to support the movement he stood for.

That is the power of symbolism when used to drive social movements. Symbols provide an association, a representation, and a narrative of the values and beliefs for the social movement community it represents. Although not necessary, mere association is key in our minds to help us think through the possibilities, the aspirations, and the hopes the social movement itself wants to conquer.

Kenneth Burke is considered one of the best rhetoricians of the twentieth century. Burke, born in Pittsburgh, Pennsylvania, was a Columbia University dropout and a self-taught scholar. He was a literary theorist focusing on analyzing rhetoric and literature from a new vantage point from what he called symbolic action. He referred to language as "a species of action, symbolic action, and its nature is such

---

[1]http://communityjournal.net/wp-content/uploads/2012/07/Martin-Luther -King.png.

that it can be used as a tool.[2] Robert Heath, in his book *Realism and Relativism,* describes the power of symbolic actions in literature that can be applied to social movements.

> To comprehend symbolic action, Burke dialectically compares it with practical action. The chopping down of a tree is a practical act whereas the writing about the chopping of a tree is a symbolic art. The internal reaction to a situation is an attitude, and the externalization of that attitude is symbolic action. Symbols can be used for practical purposes or for sheer joy. For instance, we may use symbols to earn a living or because we like to exercise our ability to use them. However philosophically distinct the two are, they often overlap.[3]

In looking at how we talk about symbols and use them in our everyday life, the general population is used to this type of rhetoric to help build the case and follow a stream of logic and support for the perspectives of the community. In essence, the symbols we have for our causes and social movements become the common set of beliefs we share as a group, the rallying cry for humanity—a humanity we perceive should be just and willing to support those who are of the community we have a connection with.

Symbols can also unite a people in a community in which differences are plenty. If there are competing causes, social issues, and ideas within a community, a symbol can break through to help unite a group and drive the association of those who share similar values. This is further explained by Burke in three major concepts that involve how symbolism can unite the voices within a community and a movement. They are as follows:

> Creating an agreement through which the two sides are united in substance (creating common ground). For example, using common ideas and attitudes based on the grounds that

---

[2]Kenneth Burke, *Language as Symbolic Action* (University of California Press, 1966).
[3]Robert L. Heath, *Realism and Relativism: A Perspective on Kenneth Burke* (Mercer University Press, 1986).

we form ourselves or our identities through physical objects, occupations, friends, activities, beliefs, and values.

Creating an agreement by way of identifying with the antitheses of a given situation. For example, if a number of people should oppose a particular issue, they can be united under the umbrella of the common enemy.

Creating an agreement by using sympathetic symbols in order to predispose an audience to the speaker.[4]

One symbol in particular has helped to bring a spirit and system of beliefs and values that Burke describes in his theories. That symbol, the pink ribbon, represents the hope and opportunity of a community in order to build a sense of association with others that share in a common belief that a cure is imminent. The pink ribbon represents the breast cancer movement globally. The Susan G. Komen Foundation first used the pink ribbon in 1991 when staff and volunteers handed out ribbons to participants attending the New York City race for survivors. In 1992, it was adopted as the official symbol of National Breast Cancer Awareness month. Since then, companies, organizations, and entities have used the pink ribbon as a uniting force for those fighting breast cancer and their families who support them.

In looking back at some of the greatest speeches of our time, you will find that the most effective ones used an element of symbolism to inspire the audience to believe and act. If you closed your eyes and listened to each word of some of the speeches from Martin Luther King Jr., John F. Kennedy, Maya Angelou, or Gandhi, you would be able to see the vision they tried to help their audiences decipher as an opportunity for the future. This is an important piece for social movement builders who want to create opportunities for people to come together. Through vision, narrative, and symbolism, a community can come together to be inspired to create and be part of the change and good the movement represents.

---

[4]http://blog.iese.edu/leggett/2012/05/17/symbolism-identification-and-kenneth-burke-2/#sthash.wpfqlxAO.dpuf.

TYPES OF SOCIAL GOOD MOVEMENT SYMBOLS

Symbols can be abstract or intentionally personal. In the abstract world, a symbol can represent a concept that defies or represents the challenge facing a population. For example, the Autism Speaks movement has centered on the puzzle piece. This puzzle piece represents "the multifaceted characteristics of autism and the diversity of the people that it affects."[5] The puzzle piece logo concept was created by the National Autistic Society in 1963 to represent the multiple sides of autism. Organizations since that time have used the puzzle concept in their logo variations to unite the autism community in support of families and individuals dealing with the condition.

Most notably in the past several years has been the symbol of charity: water. The yellow water jug provides an ongoing demonstration to those who want to provide water to so many with a connection to the organization. Rather than using the name itself, the outline of the jug and the presence of the jug in various marketing and fundraising campaigns have led to simple association to the community that follows the organization.

The yellow water jug continues to be represented not just in print and online, but also in physical objects when on-the-ground grassroots campaigns are created. The organization's annual event, charity: ball, provides an opportunity for supporters and close friends of charity: water to share in an evening of celebration and support for the cause. The use of the jug throughout the event is a symbol of what a person may receive and thus reinforces the concept of the organization and its values.

Beyond inanimate objects, some organizations use individuals to represent the movement. When an organization uses a person to drive movement building, it is for strategic purposes. The individual represents either the immense challenge the population like them needs to overcome or the vocal spokesperson for the movement.

This can be easily demonstrated through one organization in particular that used both strategies—people affected and a spokesperson. For years, the Muscular Dystrophy Association (MDA), when the MDA Telethon was at its strongest, positioned their spokesperson Jerry Lewis

---

[5] http://www.answers.com/article/361999/the-autism-puzzle-piece-logo-meaning.

with a child in all movement materials. Jerry was famous for talking about "Jerry's Kids," the ones who needed support and assistance from the general public to overcome challenges they faced with muscular dystrophy. The symbolism of his face with other smiling kids instilled within the at-home viewer or donor what is possible when support is provided to the MDA and directed to the littlest kids who need help. Jerry Lewis's imagery and likeness were used significantly throughout the past 30 years. Jerry's annual telethon was a given, and people were shocked when he stepped down from his role as emcee and lead campaigner on the Labor Day weekend show.

WHEN A SYMBOL BECOMES AN ACTION

Some social good movements have used symbolism as also part of an act—an outward sign of not mere association but an activity for the movement participants to partake in to show their support for the values of the campaign. Movember, the international movement to support prostate cancer prevention and research, uses the symbol of the mustache each November. Men are asked to grow beards and mustaches to show their support and remind their friends and family to schedule routine checks on their prostate for early detection. Although the organization could have created a different symbol or use their name as a mark, they chose to create the act of letting facial hair grow as their way to inform others about the movement itself. This strategy has created a force of men who have looked at the movement as an opportunity to outwardly show their support through a small act rather than giving money.

Another organization using this strategy is Red Nose Day. Although new to the United States in the mid-2010s with a campaign launch through a major television network, the organization has been creating waves each year in Europe through their campaign of laughter and support for hunger relief causes. Each year a community of comics, celebrities, world leaders, and more come together to show their support for hunger relief by wearing a red nose. Advertisements on air and in print show the red nose as an opportunity to remind people of what is to come with the campaign. Individuals can purchase a red nose and wear it the day of the campaign to support the cause. This simple act enables others to feel part of the movement without having to be a comic or entrenched in the hunger relief community.

DOES A MOVEMENT NEED A SYMBOL?

Today's movements don't need symbols. Historically, social good movements have used marketing verbiage to represent the story of the movement without the need for a visual cue. For example, Save the Children coined the "For Just a Dollar a Day—Less Than a Cup of Coffee" message to get the United States population to care about the atrocities occurring in Africa. With that message delivered by celebrity Sally Struthers and reinforced in marketing and print materials, people began to sign up in droves.

But is it possible today to not have a symbol? Can it be done even with a Twitter hashtag or just a word? Yes, but it is apparent that symbols today add value to the message and reinforce the movement position to converts. The movements that use words or hashtags need the opportunity to express beliefs in other ways than just through a message. Therefore, social good movements that use the act of a symbol as a rallying cry of existing supporters will find ongoing champions willing to share, speak about, and let their voices be heard with the symbol that represents their shared value with the movement.

THE HUMAN RIGHTS CAMPAIGN LOGO—A TESTAMENT TO MEMORABLE SYMBOLISM IN SOCIAL GOOD MOVEMENTS

The roots of the Human Rights Campaign go back to 1980 when it was founded to support "pro-fairness" to congressional candidates and legislatures that supported discriminatory laws and beliefs. At the time, the organization was called the Human Rights Campaign Fund and had a deep history with political action and lobbying for the rights of those being discriminated against—including LGBT (lesbian, gay, bisexual, and transgender individuals) people.

In 1995, the organization underwent a reorganization and rebranding effort to align its programs and goals at the time with the brand and likeness of the organization. The concept of being just a "fund" and political action group no longer depicted the extensive role the organization was playing in communities across the country. That year the organization dropped the word "fund" from its name and at the same time created a new logo and symbol for the movement of equality and fairness.

FIGURE 5.2   The Human Rights Campaign Symbol

As Human Rights Campaign Executive Director Elizabeth Birch would often say, "A logo is only as meaningful as the hard work and standard of excellence it represents."

At the time, the HRC leader was interested in creating a symbol and logo that fully represented the equality and vision of the organization that every person is equal in community and by law. In addition to soliciting advice and counsel from internal leaders at the organization, key stakeholders, and volunteers, Birch hired a marketing and design agency to create a concept that could depict the goals of the organization. The leadership, including Birch herself, was supportive of the equal sign concept. Although this was the internal design of choice, it didn't perform well in outside market research. After much discussion, the team at Human Right Campaign decided to move forward with the equal sign concept (see Figure 5.2). It was by far the closest to the vision of the organization going forward.

From this point on, the symbol took on a life of its own. T-shirts, stickers, and other marketing materials were produced with the new logo. New members to the organization were displaying the equal sign logo on their cars, on computers, and in offices across the country.

AN ADAPTATION SPARKS A VIRAL SOCIAL GOOD MOVEMENT

In the spring of 2013, the U.S. Supreme Court heard arguments in several marriage equality cases. The cases before the court were key to the organization's equality fight for the LGBT community. If the court struck down marriage equality, the organization would suffer a big blow to its work and campaign.

FIGURE 5.3 The Marriage Equality Campaign Symbol

At the time, the organization was looking to develop even more awareness than ever before given the importance of the cases. The organization needed a way to draw attention to what was happening in Washington. It turned to a simple variation of its logo (see Figure 5.3) and made a request of its members, supporters, and impassioned legislatures. The ask was simple: change your profile on social media—Facebook, in particular—to show those closest to you and key stakeholders in Washington that equality must win.

The organization created a red version of the logo and quite simply, it went viral. Individuals everywhere were changing their profiles to support the equality movement of the Human Rights Campaign. The color red symbolized the love we have for everyone—thus a sub-branded message reflecting the values of the organization. There was a 120 percent increase in Facebook profile photo updates as a result of the new red logo. It became a symbol for not just Human Rights Campaign members and their loved ones, but celebrities, companies, lawmakers, and anyone wanting to join the equality movement. From Beyoncé to George Takei, Martha Stewart, and Ellen DeGeneres, nationwide everyone was showing their support. Words and hashtags like "equality," "love," and "Marry who you love" were trending consistently for a week. Amicus briefs were filed by lawmakers and even by President Barack Obama to the United States Supreme Court—showing their support for striking down the Defense of Marriage Act that existed in the United States. Even companies began to show their support by displaying the red logo on their Facebook pages. Companies like HBO, Fab.com, Anheuser-Busch, and more showed their support for the Human Rights Campaign message.

The Supreme Court struck down the Defense of Marriage Act, creating the opportunity for states to broaden marriage laws to allow for marriages between more than just a man and a woman. The case was decided on its merits alone. The United States LGBT community, however, along with new allies, changed the public discourse in large part due to the simple act of a new red logo brought to the public by the Human Rights Campaign. From celebrities changing their profile picture (see Figure 5.4), to corporations incorporating the symbol on their product pages (see Figure 5.5), everyone including politicians (see Figure 5.6) were part of the movement. This alone is a representation of how a social movement used a symbol to draw action, support, and discussion among a populace usually unfamiliar with the actions of the Supreme Court and the lawmaking process. This symbol ultimately changed the way social media can be used for good—to inspire, draw

FIGURE 5.4   Social Media Profiles of Celebrities Using the Red Equality Logo

FIGURE 5.5   Social Media Profiles of Corporate Brands/Products Using the Red Equality Logo

FIGURE 5.6   Social Media Profiles of Politicians Using the Red Equality Logo

hope, capture attention and provide a community with a common act of awareness building.

IMPLICATIONS FOR SOCIAL MOVEMENTS

Symbolism draws us in and brings us closer to those who believe in the vision and story of what the people in the movement are about. Sometimes this symbol can be figurative, illustrative, or even conceptual. But the uniting power of a symbol can help those who build social movements for good create a narrative and rallying cry for those who can't do so on their own. Social movement builders need to also use symbolism because they can:

- Inspire a population to reach for something they believe in.
- Share a point of view and system of beliefs and values.
- Bring structure and identification to the group of people who want to reach for something bigger than they are.
- Build a coalition of people for the same social issue or cause in the eyes of the general public.
- Attach an ideology to a concept that some may never experience first-hand but do believe in.

Chapter 5   Creating a Movement … A Unifying Business Purpose

Jay Coen Gilbert
Co-Founder, B Lab and B Corporations

Jay Coen Gilbert and his good friends Bart Houlahan and Andrew Kassoy came together in 2006 to found what today is the B Corporation movement. They each deeply cared about the role business should play in the community and make the world better for those who work for the companies, buy goods and services, and interact within the communities where companies reside.

To say that Jay alone or Bart and Andrew created the B Corporation concept and movement would not be entirely true, as Jay would relive the early days. The founders began to interact with groups of entrepreneurs and social investors who were very interested in how their businesses could be a force for good. Through private meetings, conferences, and other business connections, they realized there was a growing community of for-profit enterprises whose leaders were yearning to come together for something much bigger than just networking. This group was looking to scale up and address some of the biggest social and environmental problems of the day, but struggled with how to make it a reality.

Jay and his co-founders realized that the community they sought to have could be formed, but it would need standards for measuring how well they were doing the good they claimed to be doing. These companies could publicly claim they were doing good or addressing a social issue without backing it up. They had no common set of standards for measuring their claims.

After creating the community of B Corporations, the founders created a set of standards of sustainability and social issue engagement for the community to measure themselves by. The goal was to tell the difference between a company that was just saying something and a company that was actually doing something. Removing this skepticism was an opportunity for these companies to show their clientele that they weren't just talking the talk but were also walking the walk.

As standards were developed, another issue arose from conversations within the B Corporation community. It focused on the need to earn capital. To earn the capital necessary for these companies to scale up and be a force for good, a new legal structure would need to be created. In the United States alone, there is a legal corporate structure that places a premium on maximizing income for the shareholders, who are the company's owners. Once capital is brought into a for-profit company, shareholders have a right to make a return on their investment. But what if a company wants to do something more? They needed some legal protection to help them focus on a higher purpose than a typical for-profit enterprise. From there, the B Corporation status and legal protection corporate structure was created and has moved into various states as a recognized entity option.

The last thing Jay and his co-founders did was create a unified brand with a unifying symbol for businesses that want to maintain a level of community and higher purpose. The "Brought to You by Certified B Corporations" symbol has become a standard for many that strive to embed doing good into their corporate movements to provide services and products while also contributing to social and environmental issues. The symbol now graces the websites, products, and services from more than 1,300 companies in more than 100 industries in over 40 countries that have been certified.

As Jay tells the story, these 1,300 businesses are not only "creating a class of companies that's more easily identifiable and therefore more easily supported by us as consumers or workers or investors, but they're also creating a much easier path for others to follow to use their business as a force for good whether or not they ever want to become certified."

Jay describes B Corporation executives and leaders as individuals who want to always do more than what they see and perform on paper. They want to make money and a difference. They want to bring their whole selves to work and be present and purposeful. They don't need to wait to make a difference after making money. It is about making money and doing good at the same time. He comments that these leaders are very resourceful. They are able to look across their product and service lines and see the social opportunities available to truly make a difference. Whether that is treating employees or their consumers better to helping a community overcome a social and civic issue, these leaders are not satisfied with just producing a product and waiting for it to make money.

Jay also sees that traditional businesses and not startups alone can take an approach through the B Corporation model. The current B Corporation created that movement alone and now companies already in existence are starting to catch the bug. What is the most interesting part of the B Corporation movement is that no matter what the size, the tools to be a company and a force for good are the same. As companies become certified, they get on a journey of self-improvement. As companies, no matter what their size, begin to increase their own standards and start to improve, they join with all other companies that are at similar stages seeking and yearning to be better.

Jay recounts the story of Etsy as an example. At first, the company was certified with a score barely over the minimum required. The company's CEO wrote a note to the B Corporation about how proud they were to now be a certified B Corporation, but they still had a lot of work to do. This was just the first step. The assessment tool became a path of movement for them and they came together to figure out how to be better. They had to answer such questions as, "Do we employ any people with disabilities?" and "Are there any jobs here that could be done by people with different abilities?" By going through this exercise and asking these questions, the company then figured out that there were such jobs, and they now employ individuals with disabilities who never would have gotten the roles without the B Corporation assessment.

To this day, Jay is surprised at how the community of B Corporations continually rely on one another and that the symbol of certification is more than just a mere opportunity to unite them all. The standards the community alone has put on themselves has truly brought this concept to where it is today. Signing and sharing their Declaration of Interdependence, one of the first steps to becoming a B Corporation, unites this group of companies in thought, theory, and practice. It brings action and purpose together, and seeing fellow companies practice what they preach in order to be an incredible movement unto themselves is important. That intentional business approach led by some incredible social and entrepreneurial leaders brings the B Corporation into a practice of doing good by also practicing what it truly means to be a business of and for purpose.

In my final question to Jay, I asked him what he wanted to be remembered for years from now. His statement reflects the community and purpose of the B Corporation movement.

> I don't care if people remember or know anything about me. Not relevant. What I hope that people remember about B Corporations is that they're a better way to do business. And if they want a society that enjoys a more shared and durable prosperity for all of us, then we'll get there further and faster if we all go to work for, start, buy from, or invest in a B Corporation.

Chapter 6 The Business of Doing Good

What is the role of business today?

The historical answer to this question was quite simple. Develop a strong business, find great people, create great products, and build profit. This equation for success was the mantra for many businesses and continues to be the genesis for success.

Is this wrong?

No, not at all. This type of approach to business has sustained companies for the long haul, weathering the storms of depressions, recessions, and cultural changes. What has been even more interesting about the historical approach to business is that although the focus has been on building an institution that generates profit and great products, there has been a lack of understanding of how that business and its products affect the local areas and communities where it lives. Moreover, there is even greater concern with how those companies treat its employees, the practices it undergoes to create those great products, and whether they are produced in a manner that hurts the environment or community where it is based. Sustainable practices and corporate social responsibility, both terms lauded to cover these areas of concern, have been at the forefront of these companies both at the will of consumers and their employees who today believe that business has a role beyond making money.

Traditional business has also stepped into the social good space by creatively using their products to support and advocate for social issues.

From changes in packaging to cause-related marketing campaigns, these companies are using their interaction with consumers as a way to communicate company values and beliefs, along with support for a cause. This approach, although controversial at times given the cause or issue being addressed, steps the company out in front of others at a time when younger demographics seek products that go beyond just their own utility but truly stand for something the individual can believe in.

In addition to what we are seeing on the forefront of traditional businesses, we are seeing other waves and practices coming out of the startup community. Founders are creating models that embed the social good concept at the core of the business. From products to services, eyeglasses to shoes, we are now beginning to see a wave and movement that makes social and good business not just about money but about helping communities, people, and causes address issues such as the environment, poverty, and social injustice. This movement, led by organizations such as B Labs, is capturing and harnessing the interest of business leaders and founders to focus on cause, social purpose, and community. Through a combination of public policy and practice, resources and networking, this community is growing and is on the verge of becoming its own movement worth noting.

These three approaches, sustainable practices, products and cause marketing, and social good businesses, are the social good movements in business today. Each of these approaches moves the company away from a private role, even if the company isn't a public entity on the stock exchanges. The companies that have embraced these approaches have helped to develop new consumer audiences, narratives about the social issues affecting our communities, and safer and healthier products for consumers. Although profits may not be realized for some companies because they take these approaches, the "warm glow" effect of the company is elevated as it becomes aware of the consumer and community, ultimately resulting in reputation-building and positivity, making it all worthwhile for both the consumer and the company.

THE SUSTAINABLE MOVEMENT

Although there are varying definitions for a sustainable business, the discussion essentially focuses on a concept simplistically stated that business practices, operations, product development, and service delivery do not impede or negatively affect the people, consumer, or community it seeks to serve. By this definition, businesses must be cognizant of their approaches and practices in an effort to ensure the consumer and the public are safe, healthy, and thriving, not necessarily as a result of the company, but because the company did not impede that success.

Some would argue, why does this matter today?

In light of technology today and consumer behavior, transparency efforts have led us to the point that the consumer's education and ability to seek and process information about products is at an all-time high. The consciousness of the brand and its products are now at a forefront more than ever before. Consumers were not historically privy to information on how products were developed or the scope of the byproducts of any good produced. In recent history, this has changed. Consumers now have advocates, not just typical watchdog groups that have always played this role, but fellow consumers today who believe in spreading and sharing knowledge about good product practices. Social networks and other platforms have been developed in an effort to inform and create a community with like-minded consumers who not only believe in such practices but want to share their experiences with products and the brand—ultimately reinforcing the notion that today's companies are not really as private as they once were.

We also see today that consumer preferences are changing. In spite of higher costs and inconvenience at times, younger consumers are willing to purchase goods that meet the standards of good, sustainable practices. Take, for example, the restaurant group Chipotle. This company's practice in sustainable food practices and ingredients has helped to propel the company ahead of other restaurant groups and chains like Taco Bell. The price point of the products as compared to their competitors is much higher but the individual consumer is willing to incur higher costs because company practice (sustainable food approaches and service delivery) combined with simple offerings (scaled-down menu options), and consumer value proposition (consumption of product is an expression of personal values) makes for a highly competitive business environment that is challenging others to keep up with.

In looking at sustainable practices and the movements created, we can categorize them into three major areas, as discussed next.

Sustainable Practice

In this area, sustainable practice refers to the operational side of the business. It encompasses the employee and internal efforts to run the business that will ensure safe and sustainable operation sites. Efforts to reduce carbon emissions at corporate headquarters, build buildings that are environmentally friendly, and create safer working environments for employees all help to build the sustainable practice of the company.

One leading movement in the sustainable practice area is the LEED certification programs as created in 1993 by U.S. Green Building Council (founded by Rick Fedrizzi, David Gottfried, and Mike Italiano). In that year, they convened more than 60 architectural firms and organizations to create a rating system for the field that balanced interest in industry with environmental building standards through a rating system. This was the predecessor to what is now the LEED (Leadership in Energy and Environmental Design) green building certification system for commercial, institutional, and residential projects that meet certain environmental and health standards in the United States. This movement now has approximately 75 chapters, more than 13,000 member companies and organizations, and 180,000 professionals who hold LEED credentials.

Sustainable Products and Services

In this sustainable business area, the focus is on creating products and delivering services that meet or exceed practices that contribute positively to the environment, community, and the people intended to benefit from their consumption. This area also includes the act of creating products that will use less harmful goods, ingredients, and chemicals in an effort to overcome any physical or social impact on the places, people, or animals used in the process.

Sustainable Community

In this sustainable business practice, companies create initiatives that will support, through advocacy, action, employee resources, and funds, issues and causes that have relevance to the company, its employees, and consumers. In this area, companies create and volunteer giving and advocacy efforts to bring attention to issues that have a connection to the product and service of the company. Companies will also create cause-marketing campaigns that will use their products and services to generate action and awareness by their consumer base. This ultimately heightens the company's and the consumer's interest in the shared value and issue being addressed.

SOCIAL GOOD BUSINESS MODELS

Newer to the business environment is the embedding of social business models for good within the for-profit sector. These companies and concepts focus on delivering products and goods that will drive attention to an issue, produce a good for an individual, and create an opportunity for consumers to not only benefit personally but also help someone else. Common practices in this approach include, but are not exclusively, the following:

One for One Model: Creation of a business model in which the consumer essentially purchases a good, and as part of the purchase, another person in need will receive a version of the product for their own benefit. Examples of this model include Warby Parker, TOMS Shoes, and Harry's.

Percentage of Sale Model: In this model, the business creates an approach whereby a percentage of the sale of the good or service directly benefits an issue or cause. This model has been effective in raising awareness about the product and good in addition to some resources directly funding the issue. In observing this model in greater detail, the cause or issue greatly benefits from the awareness-building more than it does from the financial support itself. Examples of this model include Newman's Own and Ben and Jerry's.

Percentage of Profit Model: In this approach, the business has developed within its practices and mission to give a percent of the business's profit to an organization or issue. Through this practice, we have seen several variations from the company creating a fund for employees to vote on where to give the money to a company creating a foundation led by their senior executives to create a giving approach based on statements of purpose and impact. Examples of this model include Nau and Salesforce.

Human Capital for Good Model: In this approach, a business may employ a disadvantaged population to help with manufacturing, designing, and creating a product or service. In this approach, the social good framework is based on the human capital rather than a direct financial output or advocacy effort. This approach helps to employ people who typically are not sought after in competitive hiring environments. This model has been used in the areas of development disabilities and the visually impaired such as Bosma Enterprises and Verba Voice.

Reuse and Repurpose Model: In this approach, the business repurposes goods, products, waste, and other byproducts after use to generate new goods or fulfill a purpose for the community. This business approach helps the community and environment, and helps the consumer understand the value of repurposing goods. Companies such as recycling entities and other groups such as Teracycle have popularized this approach.

All of these approaches, and others not identified here, enable the company to establish a clear message to internal and external stakeholders that the purpose of the company goes beyond profit and more to the social importance of issues and community. The movement to build this within the business approach for a sustainable model helps the company to clearly identify with a social issue that other competitors may not be able to competitively overcome.

After studying these models, it is apparent that the companies and the individuals behind them use certain tactics that go beyond just setting them up as social enterprise entities in the for-profit marketplace. In particular, after an analysis of various models, it was apparent the following also existed that helped influence both the behavior of its internal and its external stakeholders.

SOCIAL BUSINESS MOVEMENT BUILDERS

Within the company exists a socially conscientious movement builder: A person who seeks more than the typical outcomes of business and feels compelled to bring into the business model social movement building acts. This is in part due to the individual's personal experience with serving and giving to issues and causes if the individual has benefited from private philanthropic or public assistance in the past. He or she may also have had previous employment experience working in an industry and thus feels the need to change production and manufacturing methods to instill a positive impact on the community.

The social business movement builder also creates a vision for the duality of profit and purpose and helps employees and consumers alike see the importance of such practices on people and communities. The social movement builder is able to also create internal social business ambassadors able to amplify the voice of the approach to employees who do not see the purpose of such practices. These internal ambassadors and adopters of the model are able to educate and persuade employees to take advantage of the social business model that is personal to them. This includes acts such as volunteerism, skill-based community engagement, giving programs, and advisory roles with advocates.

INTERNAL POLICY CHANGES

The founders and the leaders of these companies have created internal policies that would enable employees to take advantage of social good programs offered. Policies such as allocations of individual time toward the social mission if it was not part of the individual's existing role; creation of time off and service opportunities throughout the year that incorporate company, department, and individual options; and company philanthropy and giving policies that went above and beyond incentives to support local organizations and company specific initiatives. Some companies also created initiatives that allowed employees and internal stakeholders to take advantage of unique opportunities for personal and professional engagement. Harry's, for example, created Harry's U, a program that allows entrepreneurs to take advantage of mentoring opportunities to create businesses and social enterprises by attending learning and mentoring sessions with Harry's leadership team and executives of other startup companies. In this case, employees have an opportunity to engage in the program and within the corporate culture. Policies exist to get involved if the individual seeks the opportunities.

CONSUMER COMMUNITIES FOR GOOD

Companies and enterprises with more retail operations (commonly referred to as BtoC, or business to consumer) have created consumer communities that support the social business approach to the company. These communities are built to enhance the relationship to the company by adding the purpose environment to their brand engagement. For example, companies such as celebrity Jessica Alba's The Honest Company have a large legion of parents and in particular mothers who use the product and support the mission of sustainable, environmentally friendly, and safe products. The community receives learning opportunities, tips, and ongoing educational content in an effort to help bolster the brand's social and eco-friendly mission. Doing this adds immense value and loyalty to the brand and the products.

GOVERNMENTAL POLICY CHANGE

Until recently, some companies have been focused on governmental policy change in social issues. In looking at their business models and approaches to long-term corporate sustainability, these companies have begun efforts to revolutionize a federal or local policy in an effort to bring awareness to issues in which the company or its consumers are affected. One example of this is Panera Bread. At Panera Bread, the company decided that the best way to achieve part of its social mission is to turn their skills and strengths to address societal issues. They began to address hunger as an issue because of the role their company plays in the food industry. From an interview with Kate Antonacci of Panera Cares, the social arm of Panera Bread, she commented on the reasoning for involving themselves in social policy change:

> When we first decided to address the issue of hunger in America through the development of a donation-based cafe model, there were many who told us that as a publicly traded company, it didn't make "business sense" for Panera to devote time and resources to building a non-profit enterprise. On that score, I'd argue that they were wrong. Our concept—Panera Cares—is about a conscious approach to business in which making a difference in our communities makes a difference

for our business. Panera Cares is a powerful differentiator that helps build trust with our customers and pride with our associates, and ultimately enhances our competitive advantage.

At the end of the day, unless we take care of the society we live in, there won't be any society left to support us. If we don't view our companies and ourselves as part of a sustainable model, we won't be around very long. We must give as much as we extract. Not only is it a smarter way to do business, but it's also the right thing to do.

As citizens of this world, our companies have an obligation to contribute to society in a way that goes beyond philanthropy. It's time for us all to look within and figure out how we're going to harness our non-renewable resources—namely, our time and know-how—to directly address the world's inequities. This is about taking an unconventional path to create better solutions. This is about proving that our companies can use their core competencies to make a substantive and lasting impact in this world we all share.

THE B CORPORATION MOVEMENT

In 2006, a new movement in business was formed to recognize and hold business accountable to social and environmental performance, accountability, and transparency. This movement, known as the B Corporation movement, started by B Lab, was the first time for-profit entities could be recognized and come together for the purposes of embedding social models into the heart of a business beyond typical corporate philanthropy and sustainability efforts.

Today, more than 1,000 businesses have joined a movement that for many didn't exist before 2006. Until that time, the community didn't have a leading movement builder or entity driving the social change for-profit enterprise. What B Lab has done for the movement in the United States is to organize, professionalize, and bring together founders, leaders, and their companies that seek to have a greater impact. In essence, B Lab was the catalyst and structure that the movement needed to bring these stakeholders together to build a stronger narrative nationwide for others to follow and be a part of.

PATAGONIA—CREATING A SOCIAL MOVEMENT FOR BUSINESS SINCE 1960

If there is any company that has been at the forefront of the business for social good movement, it is Patagonia. Since 1960, this outdoor adventure and retailer has created not just products, but policies and now a venture fund to create a method and purpose to its mission. What is remarkable today is that the philosophies behind the social good business created by Yvon Chouinard have not only thrived but have continued to be relevant for all generations, thus resulting in a movement of consumers and social activists who believe wholeheartedly in the power of purpose, products, and activism.

Chouinard Equipment, the predecessor to Patagonia, became the largest supplier of climbing hardware in the United States in the 1970s. The equipment provided to the field of climbing enthusiasts was praised for its durability, attention to detail, and utility. This was all apparent to Chouinard himself, who was an avid climber. As the company expanded and began to grow, it realized that a clothing line was needed, given the lack of great options for the climbing community. The clothing line launched with the name Patagonia.

From the outset, Chouinard would provide his customers with his thoughts on environmental issues. Embedded into the catalogs was editorial content about the challenging environmental issues that were occurring with pitons. Looking at the landscape of other mail-order catalogs, Chouinard was really alone in this approach. Most of the companies that had mail-order catalogs focused on selling every item to the consumer. The thought of including information on social issues was considered a wrong move. Some CEOs would have believed that the company stance in any outwardly public consumer marketing campaign and selling tool should be politically and environmentally neutral.

The approach of combining social issue coverage, activism, and consumer buying was paying off. The company began to grow very rapidly on all fronts—including the community-building areas the company began to make investments in. They were one of the fastest-growing privately held companies in the country, making the lists of magazines such as *Fast Company* and *Inc.*

Life at Patagonia, though, wasn't always perfect. The company was hit hard by the recession of the early 1990s and ultimately laid off more than 20 percent of its workforce. This was difficult for a company that prided itself on the community of employees and consumers it had built since the 1960s. What was even more challenging was that the company, for the first time, was being tested by the social policies and approaches it had implemented. Questions arose about whether such care and importance to the social mission was important, and how the doing good, building a community of consumers, and making profit could work in concert with each other to get them out of the challenges they faced.

Even in the lean years, the company decided to maintain the core competencies of its social mission. In the 1980s, they had an open cafeteria sourcing fresh, local, and vegetarian food options. They opened an onsite childcare center—at the time, they were one of only 150 in the country with one at a workplace. Today, there are more than 3,000 onsite childcare facilities spread throughout the United States. Additional benefits such as flexible time off and opportunities to learn from others such as job sharing and mentoring were givens with the company. All of these benefits, which today are a necessity for most Millennial employees, were then a nuance that some felt were unnecessary and careless corporate spending deterring from the profits the company could make.

The most significant accomplishment the company has taken has been in the approach to sustainability and the environment. Even from the early days, Chouinard and his team were not afraid to step out in front of others to make the environment a priority. They felt the environmental crisis was imperative to address because of their own experiences traveling, climbing, and outdoors adventuring.

The company not only used its marketing power to educate, but also used its checkbook to make a difference. In 1986, the company created a policy through which it would donate 10 percent of its profits each year to groups working in local areas to address environmental and habitat issues. This policy was later changed. Most would think the policy was too generous, but not the leadership of Patagonia. The amount was later increased to 1 percent of sales, or 10 percent of profits, whichever was greater. Since then, unlike other companies who have made similar commitments, they have maintained the policy and it still stands today.

The company was never afraid to take a stand on an environmental issue they felt their consumer community should address. The first educational campaign happened in the late 1980s for an alternative plan to the Yosemite Valley due to urbanization and human population interference.

Since then, the company undertakes a major environmental campaign and provides multiple channels of activism for the public to participate each year. On an annual basis, the company has made it an imperative to find that issue, generate public awareness, couple their internal resources to address the issue, and work closely with organizations on the ground that can have the most impact. By holding conferences and meetings to teach these groups how to market and build publicity, the company viewed capacity-building as an imperative to a business, cause, and public partnership in an issue to be addressed. This approach is one that some would argue is the precursor to the pro bono skills movement of today. It has helped many environmental groups they have worked with move beyond simple marketing to a grassroots network of activists.

The company has also maintained strong policies regarding its own distribution and production of products. They have reduced energy by 60 percent since the 1990s, reusing recycled content from its plants and buildings, and removing and eliminating colors and harmful dyes from its clothes. The company was one of the first to use 100 percent organic cotton in its products—something unheard of until recently for most companies in today's sportswear marketplace.

All of this has led to what has been the next stage of Patagonia's movement for good. In 2013, the company created a $20 million fund called Patagonia Works. The fund's purpose is to grow and support opportunities that combine environmental purpose with entrepreneurship. Each company supported by the fund adheres to the following policies:

- Organized as a B Corp (benefit corporation)
- Be a member of 1 Percent for the Planet
- Utilize the Higg Index or other appropriate footprint-based measurement of social and environmental performance
- Start-up or "angel" investments may be made in companies outside Patagonia Works that are not B Corporations, members of 1 Percent for the Planet or subscribers to a social and environmental performance index. But these companies must share Patagonia's core values and their work must help provide solutions to the environmental crisis.

Patagonia, throughout its history, above all other companies, has built a true social good movement internally and externally. Their founder and leadership saw early on the importance of such policies and values for their consumers and employees, and has never wavered from them throughout its history. As they continued to build this movement, the leadership of the company made concerted efforts to build upon their learning and help others in the field excel—all with an eye toward a better environment for all. This is truly a position that goes beyond social movement for good practice to true purpose and philosophy.

IMPLICATIONS FOR SOCIAL MOVEMENTS

As we look at the movement in the business community to do good, we begin to notice that the field of giving, serving, and community is not just for the nonprofit sector anymore. The field of doing good and helping others is part of the business ethos. At the core of the corporate movements highlighted in this chapter, we see that almost all of them have philosophically shifted their view on the role of any entity (for-profit or nonprofit). In essence, regardless of corporate structure or shareholder interests, it is in the interest of the many to perform ethically, transparently, responsibly, and purposefully for the betterment of others.

Whether its movements are in food security or creating a means and capacity to support local issues, companies are beginning to not just value but to depend on alternative models to generate business and enhance the relationships with consumers. With every product produced will there come another competing interest that wants to build upon someone else's expertise and product or service innovation? What sets the companies apart beyond price, shareholder value, and culture has been the companies' abilities to engage in social cause initiatives. Although there is immense value in the position of being a social business for good, the real intention and authenticity that come from that role is the memorable moment for most—including a new generation interested in not just what the company does, but also what the company stands for.

Dr. Maya Angelou said it best. "People will forget what you do, what you say, and what you write. People will never forget how you make them feel." That is the power of the social business for good we have examined. The feeling of buying, learning, and being a part of a social business and movement for good is something that no other company can replicate.

Chapter 6 Creating a Movement ... with and for Employees

Kim Jordan
Co-founder, New Belgium Brewing Company

Kim Jordan is not your typical company CEO. She has a unique background. Growing up in a liberal family, she was raised to be somewhat suspicious of profit-making, and profit motives were something to be leery of. As a social worker by trade, she started to look at profit-making a little differently. She saw a unique opportunity to use profit to advance social issues and to help employees in unique ways. She realized that New Belgium could be a conduit to address the beliefs of the employees and founders in a way that can be shared with consumers and the public.

One of the sayings that Kim has followed since her days at a Quaker high school has been "Let Your Life Speak." She has used this mantra to guide their open book management policies that allow employees to see the accounting reports whenever they want. She also sees employee ownership and their policies on energy and water conservation as all unique opportunities to let the work of New Belgium speak for itself. Through their public action, New Belgium builds a brand that engages a group of similar individuals seeking to go beyond just drinking beer.

Kim believes that the movement to do good through companies has been going on for some time. From individuals like Gary Erickson with Clif Bar to Gary Hirshberg with Stonyfield Farms, Kim finds herself in good and growing company as more and more corporate leaders see the path to great brands and products by declaring one's beliefs and values and let consumers be a part of that experience. She also believes strongly in the need to be not only a good corporate citizen but also a community builder—a role she has taken up with the social issues they have addressed. Her belief is that as the widening gap between the haves and have-nots increases, companies need to step forward and not be afraid to show support, build awareness, and drive action to address these issues. If not, she sees a community not being true to itself about what's really going on. She also sees these companies idly playing a neutral role that does not do anything for the people in their community or the profit-making company in the end.

New Belgium Brewing Company has taken certain steps under her leadership to build awareness for issues through their beer product lines. One of the most successful beer brands under the New Belgium line, for example, is Fat Tire. On Fat Tire beer bottles, a bicycle is on the front to show the company's commitment and celebration of cycling as a mode of who people are, the reduction of carbon emissions, and to address alternative options to transportation that have been part of the history of civilization. By inserting themes of their values throughout the product lines, they are reminding both the consumer and themselves of what New Belgium stands for.

But doing the right thing has been on Kim's mind since she helped found the company. This is apparent when New Belgium implemented an internal tax on itself. The company charges itself the difference between the conventional energy rate at its brewery in Fort Collins, Colorado, and the renewable energy rate. Since there is a difference between what businesses and residences pay for wind energy, the company felt that the quality of the energy the city was purchasing made it difficult to really feel enthusiastic about it making a difference. So rather than give that difference to the city, New Belgium monitored their own energy bills and every year invested in more onsite renewable energy. Why do this? Because, according to Kim, the internal practices at the company need to occur if they ever expect outsiders to follow their lead and share in the company's values.

At first, New Belgium was less interested in promoting itself and its practices. It was about living the values and not being overly preachy, according to Kim. But over time, Kim and the company's leadership realized one role the company could play is to be an advocate and tell the story of what they are doing in the hope that others will understand and join them. They started to slowly bring the concepts of their values and beliefs into their external marketing. What they found is that their consumers really enjoy that side of New Belgium in addition to the beer they drink. The company has essentially become a holistic brand offering a great product, shared values, and unique principles that help the consumer relate to them and want to act *with* rather than *for*.

New Belgium employees have always been at the core of the product lines and values system put in place by Kim and her other co-founder. From establishing its 10 core values to open management practices, employees are at the heart of the New Belgium operation. One area in particular in which this was tested was in a conversation about growth. Kim can recall the vast number of conversations about whether the company should grow. The challenges with growth for growth's sake did not entice her. But it became apparent in one conversation, after an "aha" moment, that the growth questions should not be tied to the challenges of the company to perform at higher levels, but rather about the opportunity that exists for the employees. If they were to remain at the same level, employees would be at the same position and no professional or personal growth opportunities would arise. But if the company thrived, so would the employees who are also part-owners. So growth and the decision to expand were based on the opportunities that would be afforded to the employees. As she puts it, "People who are intellectually curious and motivated to do big, interesting work don't thrive in organizations like that because it's too static. We want to continue to build a culture that has vitality and vibrancy, and that is the reason to grow, and by doing so you cultivate potential and create opportunity."

This belief in others and helping others is at the core of who Kim is. In my conversations with her, it became apparent that material things were of less interest but seeing and witnessing the happiness of employees and their success is vital. Getting to see New Belgium as a thoughtful brand in the community, standing up for the social issues that are of concern to so many, and providing support and mentorship to other social leaders in business is what drives her passion and interests. Kim sees it as being connected to something much larger than herself. The opportunity to engage with people at a level that inspires them is a powerful environment to be a part of. Fiduciary metrics and accounting are not what runs the business, and it isn't the only thing to measure. Those are functions in place to ensure the business operates with the people who care and want to take the company to another level because they believe in the power of the company as a movement and social builder.

Kim hopes that people in a hundred years will say that New Belgium was a wise and pioneering force in the area of business and social good. She hopes the company has helped change the way commerce is done in relationship to a larger and bigger context of the world in which we live. Based on New Belgium's current work in building social movements for good with employees and consumers, it seems like this will be a reality.

Chapter 7   Delivering Hope Abroad

For less than a cup of coffee a day, you can help a child.
                    —Sally Struthers, CCF Ambassador, 1987

In the travels I have made, most cause marketers and fundraisers comment on one single issue that has plagued them over the last five years, especially when the subject becomes movement building. So many wonder how and why international causes have been so successful in garnering the attention of so many people in the United States to help those overseas.

In looking back beyond the last five years, we see that international development support has been an important part of the U.S. giving culture for decades. From the early days of giving, we have discovered that so many people have been moved over the years to support causes and issues that bring water, education, basic human needs, and other support mechanisms to those who need it most.

But why, in particular, does the American public get so revved up for international causes?

In some of our research projects, we like to track the behavior and actions of some of our research participants. These subjects allow us to follow them throughout the year, see how they give and serve causes, engage with issues with their peers, and monitor their behavior and actions as they move up the engagement pyramids. During these projects, we like to ask at the beginning of the year, what kind of causes and issues they want to support in the next 12 months and why. We will also seek their opinions about the issues they find the most relevant to them in that moment and where they would like to expend their resources and energy to learn, grow, and bring in their friends to build awareness for those issues.

When we seek this input, more than 90 percent of the individuals respond with two major issue areas they would like to address, improve, and support. They include the following, in summary:

- Neighborhood: Ensuring that the place where they live is viable and safe, and the businesses and institutions within that neighborhood are supported by the neighbors and citizens who live there.
- City: Ensuring that the problems in their city such as poverty and education are addressed to ensure that everyone is able to prosper and build a successful life at home and through work.

What's missing? Helping others overseas. Almost all responses and reactions tend to focus on the challenges Americans can see in their backyard. The supports and needs they can see as they walk to get a coffee, pick up groceries, and visit the latest restaurant in the city they call home.

At the end of the year, we will look at what actually happened with their giving and service. You would think support for domestic causes and issues would be at the top of the list. But to the contrary, we find that the individual is supporting a mix of causes and issues, and international causes are at the top. In fact, some of the individuals we follow will give not just once, but multiple times to an international cause.

Why does this happen? How can so many say they have an interest in the place they call home, yet support the developing world with common basic needs and education? To answer this, we must take a quick scan and discuss the changes to the international aid landscape.

INTERNATIONAL AID HAS CHANGED

In the writing and research for this book, I had the chance to sit down and gather the thoughts and ideas of Sam Worthington, president and CEO of InterAction. InterAction is the largest alliance of U.S.-based nongovernmental (NGO) international organizations. InterAction has more than 180 members. It represents such organizations as AmeriCares and Save the Children. The work of the organization can be summed up as an educational, learning, and advocacy network for the betterment of the international aid community.

Sam's perspective on the movements created today is based on his 28 years of experience in the field. He has seen firsthand the challenges of suffering and the gap between rich and poor. Both are more extreme than most people realize. Those experiences led him to take the helm of InterAction and to guide their work to be a recognizable force with policy makers and stakeholders.

When looking at social movements it's important to note a philosophy that Sam details is at the heart of the international aid. Empathy is at the heart of the public's response in that we should all believe in our human potential. This universal approach helps guide the construct that in today's environment we are all equals and thus the disparities that exist among us should be addressed at the core level. This is not about supporting the poor or the helpless, but rather to give individuals the opportunity of humanity that they deserve.

This approach is about empathy, and it is translatable across continents. Sam further explains with this analogy:

> The neighborhood is where I live. And it represents who I am, what I stand for, and the empathy I have. And now that I am a global citizen, I have care for other areas—empathy doesn't stop when you leave the border of the United States. I have a new neighborhood today—one that exists globally, and I, as an individual, can make a world of difference if I believe my neighborhood encompasses all.

In looking at social movements today, Sam is reminded of what happened in the late 1990s. Many of the NGOs that InterAction represents came together to discover what was happening in movement building at the time and why other social issues like the environment were garnering lots of attention. These organizations came together, commissioned research throughout the United States, and realized that the social cause issue was more powerful than ever before. Rather than focusing on our individual organizations, they could create a movement by uniting for one voice. These NGOs, approximately 11 of them, came under one brand and concept. The concept was tested in Des Moines, Iowa, to understand how Middle America would react. The result? A huge, young demographic responded to the call to alleviate global poverty, and the ONE Campaign was born.

In looking at social movements, especially for international organizations, there are essentially two publics:

- The general public, which is interested in offering support based on the humanity concept discussed earlier, and
- The public of key stakeholders in the country where the work is being conducted.

Social movements in international aid must remember that key stakeholders must be involved, too. The public's involvement is necessary to show the mass support for a social issue and could tip the scales of change if the NGO is working on the ground with key stakeholders and developing the relationships necessary for potential change.

The public can be impatient when change on the ground has not yet been realized. This is why social movements with NGOs sometimes need to be carefully timed to take advantage of public interest and directed to stakeholders on the ground to overcome challenges that may be blocking change. In essence, we need movements with the public while meetings on the ground are occurring—each feeds off of the other, driving more awareness, interest, and eventual change. This was the primary reason #BringBackOurGirls struggled while the Stand With Syria campaign was more successful.

Sam thinks that social movement builders today need to think about three things when creating movements that inspire the American public to engage in international aid as a social issue:

- Focus on the inequality that exists in the world. By focusing on this as the core underpinning of any movement, the public will see and witness the disparity that exists and feel compelled to engage.
- Social movements require more than the general public. To be effective at tipping the movement forward, don't stop at just getting the public's attention. It can be exciting but distracting if there is no work on the ground, too.

- Movements are about society and the place of an individual in that society to make a difference. Remember that they are the hero in this and so is the person on the receiving end.

In the observations that we conducted with international organizations, we discovered that the approach to social movement building echoes Sam's theories and ideologies. We also discovered that there are other major components to the international aid movement that has helped bring so much attention to the American public. Here are some additional themes we continue to see.

CONTRASTING HOME WITH ABROAD

The concept of place locally is strong with everyone who has gone through our studies. As mentioned before, the individual wants to live, work, and play in a safe and supportive environment locally. The individual sees the progress and the hurt firsthand and can be emotionally invested in the success of that issue because he or she can see it.

The individual creates a picture of what an ideal place should be like based on experience, travel, and exposure to various cultures. This image is embedded in either reality or a thought that ultimately drives interest to help support that reality or thought or find ways to draw attention to it.

When an individual is exposed to images, stories, and videos that highlight the place in another country where someone is suffering or lacking opportunity, that reality and thought overcomes the individual. This results in the individual developing the urge to act in support of that ideal scenario and place.

Therefore, international development organizations and causes are fairly effective in creating a disparaging view of what life is like in a place completely foreign to the American supporter. But that view of another place in contrast to what he or she experiences on a daily basis is the relevant connection necessary to pull the empathic individual in. This results in interest in an international issue without ever having placed a foot in that country where the help is most needed.

MULTIPLIER EFFECT

In developing countries, helping an individual in need is typically cheaper than helping an individual in the United States. A dollar contributed by an individual in the United States can provide a malaria vaccine for someone abroad. Twenty dollars can cover the cost of water for one person for 20 years.[1]

We consider all of this to be a multiplier effect of aid that an individual can provide. Although some may argue that this is not an ideal support environment for those in developing countries, our argument here is based on how movements are created and supported by the public. This message of relevancy was highlighted by successful organizations like the Child Fund (formerly Christian Children's Fund, or CCF). This fund's TV ad campaign, featuring Hollywood actress Sally Struthers, described how, for less than a dollar a day, a child in a developing country could receive clean water, food, and the support he or she needed to be successful. This campaign had an immense effect on the emotional interests of the American people.

Through the multiplier effect, an individual is able to see how his or her small gifts can have an enormous effect on the individual, resulting in potential interest at higher levels. Social movements in recent history have been able to use images, social media, and video to amplify this approach to the general public. Through creative means like infographics and other design elements, an individual can see the impact of their gift on a needy recipient.

SPONSORSHIP MODEL

The first sponsorship model in international aid was created by Dr. J. Calvitt Clarke of the Christian Children's Fund in 1938. This model allowed an individual in the United States to make a personal connection to a specific child in a developing country. The sense of ownership an individual had over the support he or she could offer was immense. Individuals could realize their potential through a real and meaningful relationship with the beneficiary. In essence, the organization became the conduit between donor interest, resources, actions, and the beneficiary needing their support.

---

[1] http://www.charitywater.org/blog/20-dollars-20-years/

The sponsorship model today has continued to take shape and form, moving beyond individuals to include entities and items. Heifer International created one of the first catalogs that detailed how an individual could buy or sponsor an animal for a family or locale in another country. The purpose, as reported by Heifer International, is to pass on the gift once the livestock is received. The following is an excerpt from their website and program materials about the power an individual can have through the purchase of livestock for a family.

> The core of our model is Passing on the Gift. This means families share the training they receive, and pass on the first female offspring of their livestock to another family. This extends the impact of the original gift, allowing a once impoverished family to become donors and full participants in improving their communities. The goal of every Heifer project is to help families achieve self-reliance. We do this by providing them the tools they need to sustain themselves, and it's thanks to the generosity of donors like you. You have the power to give a hungry family the training it takes to feed themselves and their children; to give a young girl a chance at an education; to empower a woman to have a voice in her community. Together, we can change the world, one family, one community, at a time. And it all starts with a gift.[2]

Today's sponsorship model has also been digitized with new opportunities. Organizations are creating methods and ways online for individuals to see their support in real time and how their sponsorship dollars are making a difference. By using high-action cameras such as GoPros, virtual reality simulators, and live video feeds in some of the most remote places on earth, individuals can see the people and entities they sponsor and support 24 hours a day. Conservation International allows individuals to sponsor a plot of rainforest and allows the donor to name, share, and view their sponsorship in action through images and virtual or digital video.

All of these opportunities through sponsorship create a tangible ownership model for the individual. Although not true ownership, this

---

[2]www.heifer.org/about-heifer/index.html.

form of relationship helps the individual activist and donor account for their gifts, humanize the experience, and enable the emotional interests of the supporter to come to the top because the sponsorship feels real. This model, although not new, will continue to evolve and progress as organizations seek to bring donor and beneficiary closer and closer in terms of relationship and reality through advances in technology.

AWARENESS AND CAMPAIGNING MODEL

Part of the international aid and support model is based on awareness and campaigning in the United States. This approach of using tactics such as petition signing, social media, and public awareness campaigns through public service announcements or other media outlets has been used successfully to raise the public's perception and attitude toward an issue. The campaigns are based on a fundamental premise—by gathering support of the general population on an issue, policy makers and key stakeholders will view this as a sign to embark upon policy change that could result in resources for an issue. These campaigns are also designed to garner as much attention as possible on an issue through large events and campaign programs that some other traditional organizations typically don't attempt. The Global Poverty Project, for example, uses concerts, festivals, and global leader conventions for the general public to witness and experience the poverty movement from a grassroots level.

Figure 7.1 shows a graphic of the Global Poverty Project for successful and "extreme" campaigning to gain attention for the issue of poverty worldwide. The approach taken by the organization through its campaign model is three-pronged.

Impactful: The policies and practices that can achieve the greatest difference by removing barriers or creating opportunities for the world's poor to lift themselves out of extreme poverty.

Campaignable: The areas where the actions and views of global citizens can be a significant lever to change the policies and practices that keep people in extreme poverty.

Uniquely valuable: The areas where the unique efforts of the Global Poverty Project and global citizens can make a valuable or decisive contribution to changing policies or practices, given the broader political, social, and economic context of the issues.

DESIGNING & HOSTING
CAMPAIGNS
on critical issues based
on partner priorities.

CONVENING
partners & disruptive events,
together capitalizing on
influential moments &
key people.

BUILDING
THE MOVEMENT
of global citizens to
end extreme
poverty.

CHANNELING
the voices & actions of
global citizens.

Generating systematic changes that are...

BRINGING US CLOSER TO THE END OF
EXTREME POVERTY BY 2030

FIGURE 7.1   The Global Poverty Project Model[3]

This model of action through general public campaigns has also been channeled by some of the most historical organizations in the international development aid field. One historical organization, Save the Children, has taken a similar approach to campaigning in the United States through a model of mobilizing public awareness campaigns. Save the Children, started in the early 1930s, invests in the support and success of children around the globe. Through initiatives focused on bringing resources and attention to health and education, their model has helped more than 143 million children. Save the Children recently launched a new network and initiative focused on creating awareness and driving public participation to the issues addressed by the organization. The new Save the Children Action Network was established to

---

[3]www.globalpovertyproject.com/theory-of-change/.

bring the public to the issue of those unaware of it. The following is an excerpt from an interview with Mark Shriver, president of Save the Children Action Network, explaining the approach and method of the new entity's work.

AN INTERVIEW WITH MARK SHRIVER

President, Save the Children Action Network

Mark K. Shriver is president of Save the Children Action Network, where he leads an effort to mobilize Americans to end preventable maternal, newborn, and child deaths globally and to ensure that every child in the United States has access to high quality early childhood education. Shriver's career fighting for social justice in advocacy and service organizations, as well as elected office, has focused on advancing the right of every child to a safe and vibrant childhood.

Shriver joined Save the Children in 2003, serving as senior vice president for U.S. programs until 2013. In that capacity, he created and oversaw the agency's early childhood education, literacy, health, and emergency preparedness and response programs in the United States. Shriver was a member of the Maryland House of Delegates from 1994 to 2002. In 1988, he founded the Choice Program, which serves delinquent and at-risk youth through intensive, community-based counseling.

Please describe how the Save the Children Action Network movement was created and why.

> We created Save the Children Action Network in 2014 as a new advocacy arm of Save the Children, dedicated to mobilizing Americans around a commitment that cannot wait—investing in early childhood now. Save the Children Action Network—which we refer to as SCAN—was created as a bold new way to further Save the Children's efforts to transform the lives of children by working with the people who make policies that impact our children. SCAN is working to engage government officials, business leaders, and American citizens to take action and enact legislative policies that benefit children at home and around the world. To this end, we have two campaigns focused on securing high quality early childhood education for every American child and ending preventable maternal, newborn, and child deaths around the world.

What is the core philosophy behind the Save the Children movement? Has this remained constant? Has it ever changed, and if so, why?

> SCAN's core philosophy is to ensure that the issues critical to children's lives and futures are given top priority by our elected leaders and to hold those leaders accountable. SCAN will ensure that promises made are promises kept, so that all children have a fair chance in life. We share this mission with the broader Save the Children community, and SCAN now brings a different approach and area of expertise for how we're striving to reach our shared goals. The tactics may change, but our core commitment to children remains our touchstone.

When will Save the Children know the movement is a success (can be answered in both short- and long-term benchmarks)?

> SCAN has two key objectives to transform early childhood: that all American children have access to high quality early learning programs, and ending preventable maternal, newborn, and child deaths around the world. Both of these goals are ambitious but achievable. We know, for example, the most babies who die on their first day of life could be saved through simple actions such as a sterile knife to cut the umbilical cord. Here at home, poll after poll shows that Americans overwhelmingly support pre-school and high quality education. They just can't agree on how to pay for it. In both cases, we now need to harness the political will to reach these achievable goals. Long-term success is reaching the goals. In the short term, we're encouraged by progress made to further the larger goals, such as a successful ballot initiative in Seattle in November 2014 to increase access to pre-school, and world leaders prioritizing the ending of preventable and maternal deaths in discussions taking place as they craft the Sustainable Development Goals due to be unveiled in the fall of 2015.

What is the role of the individual constituent in the movement? How do they advance or strengthen the movement's goals?

> Individual constituents are key to the work we're doing. Much of our work focuses on the importance of grassroots activism, which is why we're working in several states: Illinois, Iowa, New Hampshire, South Carolina, and Washington. We

(continued)

(continued)

have staff in each of these states, and they're working directly with business leaders, educators, healthcare professionals, law enforcement officials, and religious and youth leaders who want to use their voices to effect change for children. It's impressive to see the passion of these committed individuals—and also to see the impact they have. For example, when constituents send an email or call their elected officials, it makes a difference—the lawmakers tell us they notice.

Is there a symbol, person, or entity that is associated with the movement that is easily recognizable and why? If there is, why is it so important to the movement?

Save the Children Action Network is part of the broader Save the Children movement, with offices and programs throughout the world. The Save the Children logo symbolizes Save the Children, which is a well-known and deeply respected organization that helps children around the world. Save the Children Action Network is inextricably linked with this organization, which we see as a positive. We want to show that crafting good policies that impact children is critical to furthering the tremendously good and effective [work] Save the Children has been doing for decades.

What unique and current tools or resources are used to develop interest and awareness in Save the Children?

While Save the Children works all over the world, SCAN focuses on the local, state, and federal levels in the United States, which we think is key to empowering individuals to take a stance and use their voices to effect change for children. One example of how we're working on the state and federal levels can be seen with a recent partnership we struck with a New Hampshire–based TV station, WMUR. WMUR hosts an influential interview series called "Conversation with the Candidate" where they interview each of the presidential candidates. This year we're sponsoring the series as a way to ensure candidates prioritize children and also to ensure that voters have a good sense of where candidates stand on issues impacting children. We are also conducting polls in battleground states this summer, developing political and position papers to share with the presidential campaigns and running a public education campaign to inform voters about our two key issues.

AWARENESS THROUGH PRODUCTS

Using products that directly tell the message of an issue to a consumer is a tactic international organizations are using to support the public campaigns developed. Through product inclusion and branding, the international causes have created an opportunity for the general public to be reminded of the importance of the issue. Campaigns like (RED) and FEED create products for the mass market consumer base to ultimately raise support for international relief organizations and issues. These products tend to be mainstream in order to generate the public awareness necessary for an issue or cause.

With product integration, consumer brands tend to spend advertisement dollars and support creating media campaigns to generate the attention necessary for the issue. This type of support helps the organization generate more attention than they would otherwise get with just the grassroots campaigns they have going on their own. Consumer campaigns also include in-store promotional opportunities that generate consumer experiences with the brand and the issue.

OWNING THE CAUSE

In reviewing the international aid social movements of the last five years, you will find that the marketing and fundraising leaders of the movements create campaigns for individuals to "own the cause." "Owning the cause" means that individuals can create programming, organize others, and develop their own interests through the work of the organization without prescribed actions and steps along the way. This is particularly true of causes and companies within the last five years that have established programming for constituents to develop a new approach to getting them active. Rather than creating membership models and programming, the international cause allows individuals to experience the issue with their messaging, images, and social media or other digital interactions, and then develop an opportunity for that person to create an idea that expands on his or her own. The concept of creating a message one can own versus just responding to calls to action is inherent in the way Millennials view cause and product engagement. In essence, we see the individual reacting to a set of opportunities to build a case for the support of an issue through their friends and network rather than defining how that engagement needs to occur.

This concept of "owning the cause" is demonstrated with Liberty in North Korea (LiNK). LiNK's focus is on helping North Korean people achieve liberty in their lifetime. They perform this work by working through and with Millennials on college campuses to raise support for rescues. Their "ownership" model is based on a concept of the individual choosing to make a difference and accelerating change by joining the movement of many participating in the same manner.

Through the LiNK program anyone can start a Rescue Team, which helps you develop programming at the collegiate level. Rescue teams help educate local students, participate in creative events, and develop fundraising campaigns at the local level to make rescues possible. The Rescue Team owns the relationship with the students and creates opportunities for them to organize themselves and others around the social issue. Also, the Rescue Team is based on grassroots ownership of a rescue and not on the money needed. It is all supported by the enthusiasm and will raise support for a rescue rather than setting a chapter goal that has been defined by a national organization or local level entity overseeing affiliate relationships.

IMPLICATIONS FOR SOCIAL MOVEMENTS

International social movements for good have a unique feature that can help inspire an American audience to engage with them. The inequality that exists around the world helps Americans visualize and empathize with the challenges of people around the world. But even with this important characteristic, social movement builders must work hard to double their efforts when creating movements. They need to ensure the public is involved while also driving change on the ground. Without the two simultaneous approaches, the public may not feel the change to be necessary when they participate in a movement that seems like it has vast support. Social movement building needs a goal, with work on the ground happening and the public brought around appropriately to make the goal achievable in the time frame of the movement itself.

Chapter 7   Creating a Movement … Through Fashion and Goods for the Global Explorer

Shea Parton and Raan Parton
Co-founders, Apolis

Shea and Raan Parton created the lifestyle brand Apolis for a community of global enthusiasts who were interested in understanding the globe from a different and unique angle. As global citizens, we are exposed to the real beauty, unique challenges, and opportunities that exist for all of us to be an activist and supporter of global change. Through the Apolis brand of products for consumers, there is a creative element of activism and promotion of social issues that their community can support. But what makes them so unique compared to other similar type brands? It comes down to the creative activism approach embedded in the business model and their focused management style to growth.

As global travelers, the Parton brothers were able to see so many more things than their peers. From the inequalities to the lack of economic opportunity that existed throughout the world, they believed in the need to build awareness and to try to address the challenges through a business model. In essence, making the business become a force for good. But the plan wasn't to be intentional about a movement; the Apolis business was their personal life interest because of their values. As Shea stated in our time together:

> Well we're going to do this for the next 40-plus years. We want to have something that really resonates with our quality of life, our kind of outlook on the world. It's more just … like a worldview rather than a business opportunity.

Shea and Raan have been very intentional with the products and goods that hold the Apolis name. This intention comes from the concepts of today's activist and social cause enthusiast who is now questioning the products and services of companies. They believe strongly that a business today needs to look at its products and ask some important questions like who does this product exist for, how and why does this product exist, and does it advance us culturally and globally forward? The demands from consumers, and rightfully so, should be to keep companies in line with the approach that products can benefit and fulfill a consumer need, but it cannot sacrifice global and cultural standards.

With this kind of intention in product development for the Apolis brand, Shea and Raan have built a very active and unique consumer community. The consumers who purchase Apolis products have an international mindset and awareness of global culture. They are travelers interested in exploring the globe to learn, grow, and fulfill a passion to experience other people. The consumer has a real desire to learn from other cultures and to seek out change and activism opportunities to help those locally with new and unique opportunities. The community doesn't look at a handbag as a high-priced commodity but rather at the story of its development and purpose. Shea comments that this sophistication level has changed even the way they look at pricing goods at Apolis.

> In the past, I think price really dictated sophistication. Now we're seeing that sophistication is more dictated by the level of intelligence of the brand, and we are just kind of living it rather than just talking about it.

Another business approach that has proven successful by the Partons has been a slow and methodical mentality to growth. They give credit to their parents, who had been entrepreneurs themselves in the construction business. Their father provided some unique lessons on how to move beyond the smoke and mirrors that exist in business and build a company that is based on a revenue and expense model that accounts for the hard work of selling products and creating a demand rather than trying to go after something flashy that may never amount to anything. The Partons have seen so many of their creative friends spend so much time building businesses and getting distracted by a celebrity participating in something or the next scheme to build an audience of consumers. All of this never really sustains the business, or it serves to build a consumer mentality that may not match the company's intention.

When the subject becomes doing good, Apolis has been known for helping bring awareness to their consumer community about issues affecting the global citizen. Their work in spreading information, videos, and awareness educational programming at their store in Los Angeles has become a staple of their business model. Doing good, though, was embedded from the beginning. Creating an advocacy through industry mentality needed to be included into the approach from the first day. The reason this approach was necessary on Day One was because they truly believed in the power of business for good and evolving it later into a company that focused on it after the startup phases would be too difficult.

Their view on any business being a force for good is an ideal they continue to talk about to fellow B Corporations and others interested in pursuing a social good approach to their work. They are surprised that so many want to just focus on the charitable component of giving money when so many companies have bigger assets to provide that are usually unused on social issues. They still look at charity as important for businesses to pursue, but not every business can give every dollar or a percentage of sales to the community. For some businesses, the concept of purpose-driven work can be educational and supportive of issues through employees and consumer engagement. This can have just as much meaning as giving away money.

They have viewed their work in educating and mentoring fellow social entrepreneurs and B Corporation leaders as a privilege. They see so many individuals hungry for knowledge around this area of social good and business. One thing they continue to address with these individuals, though, is that what they need to learn will take time to truly understand and that success doesn't come overnight. An example they like to give to budding social entrepreneurs is that providing good things for the community like charitable gifts or documenting a mission trip is great, but how does that relate to your purpose for being and business? How does that advance us all? Is it more about you and fulfilling your personal needs or checking off the box that you have these opportunities? In essence, being purposeful requires real intention that isn't manufactured overnight; it is part of the being of the people and the company itself. That's what makes the company valuable.

Their creative business model is based on advocacy through industry. They believe strongly that businesses can transform and address global issues when business, consumers, causes, and the public come together. It is about businesses being mindful of an opportunity to create change and embarking upon what can happen when they fully bring into their corporate ethos the concepts of globalization and mindfulness. Whether you are a big employer or a small one, every business can play a part for good in the world they call home.

Chapter 8   The Creative Behind a Social Movement for Good

I was visiting New York City for a conference to talk about the latest research we had just released. I was scheduled to go on stage around 2:00. I arrived a little early and had the chance to walk around, check out the latest exhibits, and get the vibe of the conference. This is something I like to do even before checking in. Doing this helps me understand what I may be dealing with that day.

As I was going through the area, I noticed a couple of tables off to the side. Three people were camped out next to some outlets trying to get any little bit of electricity they could to charge their gadgets. I was in need of some, too. But, of course, there were limited amounts of actual outlets.

As I was doing the walk by, a conference attendee could tell I was really in need of some charging. I was trying to look in and around the floor to find anything at this point. The attendee gave me a sign and waved me over. I came over and she said, "Do you need to charge? I can charge my phone in my laptop. It just means we have to share an outlet—if you don't mind that I sit next to you." So I did just that and nestled up to the wall and outlet close enough to her that I could see what she was doing.

She was watching some video. I couldn't really tell what it was and I was really focused on looking over a few things before I made my presentation. She participated in some small talk before I got settled, but was fairly intent on watching whatever was captivating her attention.

I was about five minutes into writing some emails and prepping when I noticed that she was now really paying attention to the screen. She was watching another video. This time I could tell she was really into the information.

So I said to her, "I can't help but notice the videos you are watching." She should have told me to mind my own business, but she didn't. She looked at me, and said, "I know. I was in this session and someone played this video from the Girl Effect. Do you know them?"

Until then, the Girl Effect was never on my list of causes or organizations that I followed. She then leaned over to show me her screen. "You have to take a look at these videos. I am mesmerized by them and what they are saying. I have watched, like, two or three since I sat down. I love what they are trying to do."

She took off her headphones and I could now hear the video for myself. It was amazing. The videos contained a sequence of cartoons. The professional term is kinetic text, which transforms text as the story is told. The narrative had nothing to do with what the girls do from nine to five, but rather it showed the importance of a girl. As a father of two little girls, my interest was even more piqued.

So I sat there for another five minutes, doing exactly what she was doing. Watching intently. Hanging on every word, every movement in the video that made my heart ache more for the challenges girls face in communities everywhere. As the video ended, we kind of looked at each other and said, "Wow." I was impressed. Not just with what they were saying, but the fact that the video was more than three minutes long. How was it possible that it kept my attention for so long?

I went immediately to their website. I had to learn more about what they do. The interesting part of the video is that it didn't specifically talk about what they did. It talked about what they stood for. The fact that girls can't be ignored.

I headed over to their site and was blown away. I think the most impressive thing was a homepage that had a huge statement on the front with two big buttons. The statement read:

Do you think the world needs a big kick in the pants?

Below this statement was two buttons—Yes or No. Well, that caught me off guard. How could I say no? I mean, I believe the world could use a big kick in the pants. And also some other people I know.

I clicked on the yes button and it took me to a declaration of the movement's thoughts and beliefs about girls. By that point, it was truly fascinating how much time I was spending on this site. I was supposed to go on stage in an hour or so, and this was not in my plan for the day. But how could I ignore this?

On the site, I saw probably one of the strongest statements that I had read in a long time. Girls Are Impossible to Ignore. That was it. The beauty of what I was reading and seeing was so simple—clear statements that spoke to me as a human being and father of little girls.

I read more. More and more sentences with simple design started to highlight the importance of the issue. Statements such as:

Girls Are Agents of Change.
Excluding Girls Is Costly.

I continued to look at their take action areas and what they offered. Most of it was centered on the notion that one can be an investor in the untold, positive story of girls and what is possible. I was moved and learned so much. Something I didn't realize at the time was an intentional goal of the Girl Effect movement builders and their creator, the team at Nike. The head of Nike's Foundation, Maria Eitel, made the following comment in an interview about the GirlEffect.org website:

> Adolescent girls have been invisible for a long time, so the first thing is really just this issue of finding ways to show the world why we need to invest in girls. That's where we were three years ago when GirlEffect.org was originally launched. At that time, we were putting a lot of effort into getting girls on the global agenda because they weren't on the radar of the CEOs, government leaders, and other influential people.
>
> The other thing is that the issues are very complex. We could talk forever about the data and programs and the factors that influence girls' trajectories, but we were missing the tools that could help people take the first step in just understanding why this is so important to all of us.[1]

---

[1] www.huffingtonpost.com/rahim-kanani/nike-foundation-girl-effect_b_850551.html.

WHY CREATIVE MATTERS

As we know, based upon previous chapters, humans are empathic and need motivation and inspiration to engage in movements and especially to be part of movements long-term. That inspiration and motivation come from a narrative and images we attach to the movement's core values and beliefs. It is the story of the person being challenged, not able to seek the opportunity that should be afforded to them, and the potential ahead of them. For this reason, the creative we surround the movement with is vital.

In looking at some of the most successful social movements for good, the creative was used to spark involvement by some clear strategies and approaches that have been used to generate the success they have had. The strategies and approaches have been the support for movements to gain traction, although on their own, not the linchpin that made the movement itself. This is important to understand, as movements require more than just great-looking creatives to be successful. It is a combination of creative, message, people, and activism together.

MOVING PEOPLE THROUGH EXISTING ACTIONS

The behavior of people is hard to change. Although individuals are empathic toward causes and social issues as discussed in earlier chapters, changing their cause behavior can take time, and the public's participation in a new act or something outside the norm is a hard habit to break. Successful movements make the act of doing good part of what the individual already does. Performing simple acts that are already consistent with one's existing behavior is not as hard for the individual to maintain. If there are social levers that are consistent to remind one to change one's behavior for good, a result can be much greater than one that asks the movement participant to consistently be mindful of his or her own behavior. One of the most successful social movements that used this concept to their advantage was the UNICEF Tap Project.

The Tap Project was created in 2007 in response to the growing challenges of clean and safe water in parts of the world where it doesn't exist. Historically, World Water Day provided an opportunity to generate awareness about the need for people around the world to have clean water. Although the day existed, a broad public awareness campaign had not been in place to attract the attention that was necessary to make it important to be addressed by the general public.

UNICEF was looking to create a new campaign to heighten interest in the water issue. They knew it had to be much different than ever before. It had to get to a place where so many people experience water, take it for granted, and be consistently reminded of the need that exists. With the help of a New York City–based agency, Droga5, the concept of the Tap Project was born.

When the creative team of the agency was out on a lunch break, the concept came to them. As the team was getting seated at their table, a server came over and brought glasses of tap water for the group. The water was free. That was when the light bulb went off. Free tap water is just a given now when you go to a restaurant. But for individuals in developing countries, this is not even in the realm of possibilities.

The team started to discuss the methods and approaches to the campaign. It would be simple: just ask people to purchase rather than accept a free glass of water. Their purchase for just a $1 would help support a person's clean water needs in a developing country for roughly 40 days. The concept was about branding the one thing we take for granted in an environment where asking for a small donation would not be a hindrance, given the average transaction amount that occurs in restaurants. In essence, the group was branding the tap water they were receiving and giving it a thoughtful and thoughtless simple act of giving. The extra $1 placed on their bill would be likely so minimal that the diner would not think twice about the opportunity.

The hardest part of the strategy, though, was the activation. How do you get people, like servers, to participate in this simple act? How do you get their bosses to allow it to occur? This may be a difficult exercise given that restaurants use computer systems to track orders and perform transactions.

The campaign's energy focused on getting some of the most influential chefs and restaurateurs in New York City to participate. Through meetings and discussions with these stakeholders, it became clear that their support and offering would bring in other owners and chefs—it became a situation of who wouldn't want to participate.

UNICEF and the agency creative team went to major media outlets and magazines that spoke to the restaurant community. Partnerships were established with entities and pro bono ad space was given in support of the campaign. When the campaign got bigger and bigger, UNICEF and their creative team went to other agencies in other cities to seek their support. The campaign was beginning to go viral from the pure fact that clean water, no matter how you look at it, is taken for granted and needed support to be successful. Being proprietary in the creative and the approach wasn't necessary for it to truly grow and build the impact it intended.

In the first year, the Tap Project's activation occurred in 300 restaurants. That year, more than $100,000 was raised for the Tap Project. That was 100,000 glasses of clean, free water consumed in support of the campaign. Since then, the project has yielded more than $3 million in support for clean water initiatives.

Why did it work? Quite simply, the campaign was an easy action for those to take. There is also is an element of peer engagement with those at the table being asked to pay for their tap water. At such a low barrier to cause involvement, the act of donating a dollar was something that could at least show one's small value and interest in the campaign.

In terms of the creative associated with the campaign, the agency effectively branded the concept of tap water. The creative team was able to take advantage of a commonly used principle when people go out to eat. The general public's interaction was already established when they latched on to tap water and it didn't require much education to understand what the brand was. Also, the creative elements in print and online made the "tap water" concept seem so clear and clean. This depicted the opposite effect in Third World countries—again reinforcing the brand of the campaign in an easily understood opportunity.

REAL PEOPLE INSPIRE REAL MOVEMENTS

The cause world is about real people. Organizations are built to serve and support the challenges real people face. They provide a donor with opportunity and a platform to succeed. This is the heart of the do-good space and speaks to the empathic heart of the population that is moved to act.

In looking at campaigns of the last ten years, the field of cause creative has been the most effective when real people represent the challenges of our time and how real people can move to make a difference.

Campaigns that we have analyzed in the past that contain any of the following elements tend to lack the emotional connection necessary to move beyond simple awareness through some small sharing acts:

- People's faces aren't included
- Outdated imagery is not reflective of the time
- Real people making a difference for the issue are missing
- Video content focuses on the organization instead of the individual being helped
- Images tell the story of a crowd and not the narrative of the individual
- Messaging speaks to an issue that does not affect a person

One campaign that took the strategy of real people to the next level to create a social movement was actually created by a for-profit and not a cause. You may have seen it everywhere, and it probably shocked most of us at the time because it was completely out of the ordinary from what the general public was used to seeing in advertisements and campaigns. This campaign was about real people and "real beauty"—thus starting to change the narrative on what constitutes beauty in the public's eye. This is the Dove Campaign for Real Beauty.

The campaign concept actually began from a research approach and not necessarily a creative team coming up with the concept on their own. At the time, there were studies performed to understand the challenges women were facing with their bodies and self-esteem. In those studies, what was apparent was that a significant number of women would not define themselves as beautiful. In fact, only 2 percent of women around the world would describe themselves as beautiful. Because of this, women and girls are challenged daily with self-esteem issues, feelings of worth, and whether they can maintain the public's standards placed upon them. What was even more telling is that the same research found that women felt they were responsible for influencing their own beauty however they defined it.

The campaign's first start was in Toronto. On a very busy intersection, in a very popular area in the city, a billboard was placed that pictured three normal women. In fact, the location was chosen because, with its particular traffic patterns, having a complete standstill at any given moment throughout the day would not be surprising. The ad featured three women with two simple checkboxes. Were they fat or fit? Gray or gorgeous? Wrinkled or wonderful? Besides the checkboxes and the image of real women, there was nothing else except a line that read:

Does true beauty only squeeze into size 8? Join the beauty debate.

Individuals could text in their vote. At the time the ad was there, 52 percent of the respondents said fat and the opposite mentioned fit. Not surprisingly, this was an issue that was going to take some more discussion and attention to truly help women.

One item quite interesting to note about the campaign was that it never featured a nonprofit cause or entity to support. This was not cause marketing but rather a social issue awareness campaign the company felt it and its beauty brands could get behind.

Since that first ad appeared in Toronto, and later in other global cities, it had a dramatic effect. Videos about the campaign featuring real women redefining the definition of beauty, were now being seen on buses, on TV shows, in magazines, and on YouTube. The campaign concept was out there, and TV talk shows were now talking about beauty issues with women. The conversation about self-esteem, beauty, and women was occurring at a pace that no one predicted or had seen in any other social awareness campaigns at the time.

The Dove brand was living the true values the general population was seeking to align with. The campaign worked because so many people have felt or discovered that inner challenge of being a beautiful person. The campaign activated those emotions, and the movement was built.

Comments from consumers were overwhelmingly positive, and they saw the real advantage to the role Dove was taking in starting the conversation throughout the world about inner beauty.

> We found out that the women and men exposed to [the "Campaign for Real Beauty"] became much more interested in buying anything the brand was selling.

> That wasn't about, "I'm so glad they put this in the shampoo." That was about, "I really appreciate what the brand is doing in the world. I want to put my dollars against what they are doing."

Dove showed what's possible when a brand decides it is hell-bent on making a positive impact and it was a demo of how much that resonates with consumers.

And what we have seen since is [that] consumers have started to expect that these corporations will use their energies toward doing good. It's become a new behavior.

As the campaign began a movement, Dove started the Self-Esteem Fund to give additional support to the social issue. This entity was created as a means of linking their support for the issue they were spending their creative and marketing dollars to address. The fund educates girls and women on the concepts of real beauty and how to build self-esteem in everyday lives. Later, Dove would align itself with charitable organizations including the Girl Scouts, Girls Inc., and the Boys and Girls Clubs of America to further deepen the movement with the women and girls they help. More than 7 million girls are now affected and supported through these programs and the Self-Esteem Fund.

Why did it work? The Dove Campaign for Real Beauty sparked a conversation so many people were feeling but never had an outlet to express themselves through. The campaign creative told the story of real beauty beyond the typical image that so many were used to. It established a new paradigm in our personal beliefs. The campaign was about a social issue, not a cause, but the real people who look in the mirror and lack the self-esteem they need to be successful. This campaign was about real people, waiting for a real conversation to occur—and a brand made it possible.

NOT TALKING DOWN TO AUDIENCES

In looking at campaigns that have started movements, it's important to note that the most successful ones use a strategy of opportunity and not talking down to the intended audience, even if that audience is the one that needs to change. Social movements can take two approaches—talking about a social issue that helps the audience understand the complexity of an issue or degrading the issue by choosing to add shock with little to no substance. The ones that choose to lightly educate an audience to act in a small way, progress toward behavior or societal change, or inspire an audience to do things differently.

Creative approaches that level all audiences and uplift each individual to create or be a part of change is a long-term approach to social movement building. Leveling the audience, making a donor at $20 or a donor at $100 equal in the eyes of the campaign, can have an uplifting effect on anyone willing and wanting to support an issue. Similarly, if the campaign helps the audience understand that everyone can be affected, or the people you are with can be affected and this is how you can be a part of the opportunity to change, is a position worth noting. The following gives examples and contrasts between creative approaches and themes that an organization and movement builders should consider applying to their creative development.

Leveling Audience Statements

Do you know someone affected by cancer? Cancer doesn't discriminate. Your friends and family can be affected regardless of whether you make $10,000 or $10 million this year. Here is how you can change the course for your friends and family.

Knowing you have a mentor to help you conquer the world is an amazing experience. Anyone can be a friend and mentor if you want to be the one willing to show a little light to those who need a little direction.

In the preceding statements, the focus of the content and development of creative themes is on the leveling of the social issue for all. It can be impactful for anyone and relevant to anyone's personal or professional career. This is an issue that transcends class, education, and income.

Talking Down Statements

If you believe that children are the greatest, then why haven't supported the National Children's Organization?

This issue is the most pressing of our time. It is just waiting for you to stop it from affecting us all.

What is the greatest thing that could happen to you today? Start something to make a difference.

In each of these statements, the tone and theme of the content is focused on the lack of participatory behavior by the audience. The rhetoric is off-putting and challenging to get motivated to partake in action with the social issue or movement because of the context of inaction and disinterest by the potential activist. This type of message may gain attention, but it lacks the buildup of interest from the individual as a hero in the scenario of the social movement's creative.

One of the most notable campaigns in recent history that didn't talk down to audiences, given the sensitivity of the topic toward a very young demographic, was the Truth Campaign by the American Legacy Foundation. The American Legacy Foundation was the recipient of the tobacco company settlement with 46 states. The foundation was charged with creating a teen anti-smoking campaign with the money it received from the court case victory.

In designing the campaign, the creators pointed to research that unveiled the reason why young people were smoking. The research stated, "Although youth were aware of the deadly nature of cigarettes, they were attracted to smoking as a tool for rebellion and empowerment. The Truth campaign designers wanted to counter the appeal of cigarettes by encouraging teens to rebel against the duplicity and manipulation exhibited by tobacco companies."[2]

From there, the agency team chose not to talk to teens as doing something bad but rather to inform them of what is happening and how they can skip the smoking opportunities that might be presented to them. One of the most aggressive of the campaign's TV spots and PSAs was the Body Bags short. The campaign brought to the doorsteps of the big tobacco companies 1,200 bags to show the deaths that occur each day from smoking. This was later portrayed by another campaign featuring youths falling to the ground with one individual standing in front of a tobacco company's headquarters.

The goal of the campaign was to help youth identify with the campaign and the brand of the campaign rather than being talked down to. It was about youths and their peers going against the tobacco company, and not an adult telling them what to do. This approach of peer modeling and modeling of behavior was one of the campaign's strongest strategies. It, in essence, allowed the audience to decide how they wanted to address smoking given the knowledge they had about the facts. This opportunity,

---

[2]http://cancercontrol.cancer.gov/Brp/tcrb/monographs/19/index.html.

to make a choice to be a part of a revolution and movement, is something social movements for good can emulate.

Did it work? Given the amount of money put toward the campaign and the creative needs necessary to reach young people, the American Legacy Foundation was under a lot of scrutiny to perform and reach its goal of preventing teen smoking. More studies have been performed to see the real impact of the campaign, the most of any social issue campaign to date.

In 2009, the American Journal of Preventative Medicine published a study measuring the effectiveness of the campaign in more than 200 media markets. The study found a direct association between youth exposure to "truth" messaging and a decreased risk of taking up smoking. Results demonstrated that during its first four years (2000–2004), the Truth Campaign prevented approximately 450,000 youths nationwide from initiating smoking.[3] In another study, researchers wanted to understand the economic impact of the Truth Campaign. It was discovered that the campaign saved between $1.9 and $5.4 billion in medical care costs to society between 2000 and 2002. In this way, the authors argue "truth" is a cost-effective public health intervention.[4]

In a goal to maintain truth's effectiveness, the new campaign in 2014 is focused on helping teens stop smoking by letting them be the hero in the social issue movement, creating an opportunity to end it, and making change permanent. This positioning is starting to work, too, as early results see a continued decline in teen smoking.

IMPLICATIONS FOR SOCIAL MOVEMENTS

Sharing messages, spreading opportunities for change, and being a part of something bigger takes a message, a sender, and the ability to feel like you can truly make a difference. Social movement builders need to help the audience understand their opportunity and power to change all while not degrading the audience itself or separating them from others

---

[3] www.ajpmonline.org/article/S0749-3797%2809%2900074-9/pdf.
[4] www.ajpmonline.org/article/S0749-3797%2809%2900075-0/pdf.

because of a lack of involvement. Positioning creative to show and help the individual partake in action that matters should be the goal of any creative design team associated with the social movement. This means going beyond just design to the concepts behind the social movements itself. Creating a narrative that makes anyone the master of the movement through their actions is the power of a strong social movement and the opportunity creative can have to move people from inaction, to understanding, to participant, to organizer.

Chapter 8   Creating a Movement ... Through Messaging and Action

Joe Rospars
Co-founder and CEO, Blue State Digital

The methods and approaches to today's cause activist can be tied to what occurred in 2008 and 2012 with Barack Obama's historic presidential campaigns. Individuals found themselves being hooked by emails with pithy subject lines such as "Hey there" or "I need you." They featured videos and images, short text statements, and calls to action that were personalized beyond just using someone's named—but based on the individual's action. The emails focused on always bringing one action or ask to the next level, small act to small act. At the end, individuals couldn't help but have given large amounts of money, performed more acts than they ever imagined, and shared content they never would have had they not been led by the powerful engagement team behind Obama's digital campaign team.

That team was led in part by Joe Rospars, the co-founder and current CEO of Blue State Digital, the digital engagement agency behind Obama's successful approach. Today, Blue State Digital has done some incredible things for clients such as the NAACP and a small organization working to challenge the British National Party. The success has been remarkable as Joe and his team continue to drive people to act for social issues today. I had the opportunity to spend some time with Joe to get his thoughts on today's social movements and where he thinks companies and causes need to spend time engaging individuals online to harness great change.

Joe defines a social movement for good today as a mechanism representative of a critical mass of people's passion channeled in a way that produces the desired outcome. Ideally, that outcome is change or some sort of prudent point for the power of that cause or issue that is greater than the status quo expectation before the movement. These movements will also move beyond awareness, which is an easy metric and one everyone wants: to truly change. Where one can be part of that change is transformational, not only for the organization, but also for the individual.

Since the 2008 campaign, Joe has realized that what was done for the Obama campaign is not necessarily the reality for most organizations. When he started working on the Obama campaign, he and his staff built the digital platform of engagement from scratch. Although the candidate had at that time a following, it was not where it needed to be to garner the attention and movement they were seeking to win an election. But not every legacy institution, as he calls it, has that opportunity. They don't have the chance to build from scratch and start fresh with a new message. There are individuals, constituents, and donors who know about them already that don't need to be ignored—but instead brought into a new ecosystem. These organizations have it tough, because what made them so relevant at the time is not as relevant today. This is the challenge that Joe and his team find themselves in today while trying to help so many organizations. What was performed in the past was great, but today requires a new message to get the activist excited about what is the most pressing now.

Joe believes that these organizations are truly valuable and were obviously founded for a reason. These organizations, though, should not give up on that journey of creating the movement today that is what their organization was founded on. He further explains to me in the following excerpt:

> The built-in community, brand positioning, expectations, reliability, and reputation of the existing legacy organizations, these are valuable things that are worthy of transformation. We (organizations, leaders, and activists alike) have to do the hard, sometimes frustrating, and slow work to transform the organizations because they're valued and have purpose.

This transformation as Joe describes it is an intentional and methodical process. The movements of today require us all to be collaborative with all stakeholders and not just the leaders, largest donors, and most active constituents. The culture of movements today is about the individual rising up and being able to be part of something. To believe in the movement, he says, is a retention strategy that needs to be built upon. Joe comments that this was a notion somewhat addressed in the past, but never really dealt with like we have to today. He feels this to be so because the technologies present today are making it possible to put individuals at the lowest end of the giving or activism spectrum right up there at the highest end of the giving and activism spectrum.

Joe realizes, though, that digital engagement can be limiting. Even with his work with the Obama campaigns and the other organizations he has helped to create change and movements for, he realizes that digital engagement can be the glue that will help pull people to action. But there needs to be an intentional strategy, at some point, to perform other work to support the digital platform. From handing out leaflets door to door to campaigning at a grassroots level, digital works best when coupled with other strategies.

During the conversation, Joe brought up several key points about digital campaign stories that resonate with the thinking of other social movement builders. He stated that the general public is very active in social issue discussions and policy problems or opportunities. But what gets lost in that discussion is the story about the person who is affected. In essence, he calls this the reality of the end outcome of a policy, the real narrative around the individual who can't receive a benefit or an offering because of a life issue. All of this is real: That is imperative in the creative story discussion that tends to be overlooked, and it is a great opportunity for so many.

Joe sees empathy as a key component to driving change, but that empathy is really a connection to someone who is as empathic as that person is. The peer relationship can go beyond just getting a friend to react to something; it can be really getting a friend who shares in the empathy and passion for an issue. Joe believes strongly that when people are empathic together, that is truly the glue of a social movement. That is the power of when a movement transcends the power of any individual who cares to a mass of people who want to "move the needle together" through a shared belief and empathy to help that individual be better in some remote part of the country. He further explains that this is what the under appreciated part of movement builders in society today really need to recognize.

> We hope the default in the future is for action to be taken by peers together who share the same beliefs. Wouldn't it be great if society today treated getting involved in movements as the norm? That the default expectation is that you act, organize, and join others? That you are not alone, that others are with you, and this is the common stream of actions we all take. That is where we can and hope we can get to. When you see an issue, you gravitate to others who believe with you, and organize with you, and yearn for that moment when change is in the midst of being realized. How moving that can be.

In the end, Joe believes in the power of a traditional ladder of engagement—moving people upward through small actions to larger actions. He also believes that technology is changing today's activist and social issue enthusiast with activities and participation in that traditional ladder of engagement. As we finish up our discussion, he makes the following comment about engagement today and the intersection with technology to transform movements.

> The evolution of user behavior makes today's activist enter that ladder of engagement differently. It isn't better or worse; it is different. We should not, as social movement builders, determine whether we think that is important or not, but rather recognize it and support the individual who believes it is important. The potency of a movement depends on a series of occasions for the individual wanting and yearning to be part of something bigger than themselves at every step of the way. Lead people there. In the spirit of the movement itself, the people who are part of it will really appreciate it when you reach the goal together.

Chapter 9 Bringing a Social Movement for Good to a College Campus Near You

At the age of 13, a young boy from Kokomo, Indiana contracted AIDS from contaminated blood transfusions he received for hemophilia, a condition he had had since birth. His story gained national attention when his school banned him from attending because of the fear of AIDS and other students contracting the deadly disease. Little was really known at that time about the disease, and fear was running rampant across the country. Individuals didn't quite understand the issue enough to understand that the disease cannot harm people by simply being in one's presence.

The boy, Ryan White, went to court to fight his school district for the same education his friends were getting. The court battle captured the attention of many people nationwide. His family was under immense stress because of the public's lack of understanding of the disease. The public directed their anger toward the family for standing up for the rights of those who couldn't. Ryan and his family moved from Kokomo to Cicero, Indiana with the hope of getting a new start on their life.

Unfortunately, Ryan's health continued to suffer. On April 8, 1990, Ryan White passed away at the age of 18. His death happened before he was able to attend the college of his dreams—Indiana University.

Jill Stuart was a little girl when she met Ryan and her new Cicero, Indiana neighbors, the Whites, for the first time. She recalls how mesmerizing his personality was. Instead of focusing on his own challenges, he was always worried about other people and their concerns. Jill and Ryan would carpool together to school each day, and she would even attend his medical appointments with him. She also traveled with him to public appearances and other events to bring friendship and support for him as he told the stories of his own challenges and caring for people who were different. She even played school with Ryan at his house.

Ryan's death hit Jill hard. As one of his closest friends, she was looking for a way to memorialize him and honor her friend. In 1991, she was a sophomore at Indiana University (IU), an active member of the Beta Chapter of Kappa Alpha Theta, student body president, and considered a leader by all who knew her. She knew one thing for sure: that she missed her friend Ryan, who was to join her as a classmate at IU that year.

Then, Jill had an idea. She was familiar with Dance Marathon concepts from other schools and was interested in creating a fun all-night event to raise money for kids like her friend Ryan. She was committed, and the first IU Dance Marathon was born. Jill described what she calls an "awful" experience that year.

> The 112 dancers were losing energy, and food had run out. People were tired. Students in charge of boosting morale brought a blow-up dragon for entertainment. One dragon, one switch, and the gym became dark. The electricity had gone out. But, they were able to survive the first Dance Marathon, raising $11,000.[1] That night they also started a fire that almost burnt down the field house. History was definitely made.

At the next year's IU Dance Marathon, students raised more than $23,000. The following year, more students came out, and they were able to raise more than $63,000. The Dance Marathon concept was proven successful, and Jill was helping to make it bigger and bigger each year.

---

[1]http://newsinfo.iu.edu/web/page/normal/12496.html.

Then in 1994, Children's Miracle Network visited with Jill and the leadership team of the IU Dance Marathon. Their goal was to talk with the founder, learn how the concept caught on so quickly, and was successful on campus in raising so much money. Through a series of conversations and discussions between Children's Miracle Network and Jill, all parties agreed to spread the Dance Marathon concept to other college campuses. The University of Iowa, University of Florida, Bowling Green State University, and Florida State University held their first Dance Marathons in the fall and spring of the 1994–1995 academic years.

The Dance Marathon movement quickly spread to more campuses, and by 2002, there were more than 50 universities participating. They were all raising support for FOR THE KIDS—the motto of the Dance Marathon movement. Today, the Dance Marathon movement represents thousands of students at more than 250 campuses across the United States joining to raise more than $25 million each year.

The first Dance Marathon mission statement from Indiana University still speaks to the power of the movement across campuses and why it is imperative for the children they help.

> Dance Marathon will be the beginning of a tradition at Indiana University. We will dance every year until we don't have sick children. We will dance every year so that the children at Riley can enroll at IU and dance and help other children who will be cured in the unit we establish. We will dance every year so that when you stop dreaming, you can come to Bloomington, Indiana, and see what happens when a few people get together and dare to dream. We want you to understand the magnitude and passion behind this marathon. We would like you to help us raise funds to develop this unit, and we would like to inspire you to dream and participate in the fulfillment of dreams.

THE CAMPUS—PERFECT SETTING FOR A MOVEMENT

The college campus today represents a setting prime for social movements. Colleges have played a historical role in forming the movements we witness today. From student activism to protests and movements, colleges become a hotbed of activity for students and young people to voice their opinions in the eye of expression and social interests.

At a time when students and young people are the most optimistic about their role in the world and in the community, there is a unique opportunity to believe in the concept of being a change maker for good. In a featured piece published in *The Atlantic*, Angus Johnston, a history professor at the City University of New York and a specialist in student activism, comments that when someone is in college, it is a time of discovery and potential. He further comments that the "belief that you can change the world [hasn't been] beaten out of you yet."[2]

The campus environment has procedures and policies in place that allow for easy organizing. Specifically, campus policies allow for individuals to form groups easily and to enable such organizing to get the recognition necessary to reap the benefits of clubs and other student organizations on campus. Campuses provide very strong protections for freedom of expression and allow students to explore their interests in a way that allows for those who are passionate to create their movements on campus. There are resources there at their disposal that other social movement builders need to expend when bringing people together. On-campus movements are able to organize a rally with fellow students who are already there with them—an environment that outside the campus is hard to replicate. Johnston further explains this in his comments about the university as a place for organizing:

> The university is big enough to matter but small enough to have an influence on. It becomes a site of organizing because there are opportunities to organize on campus that a lot of times you don't have in an off-campus community.[3]

The campus setting provides students with a unique and new experience that, for the most part, many of them have not yet been exposed to. During the college life cycle, these individuals are experiencing life on their own for the first time, being positioned by others to care for certain issues that go well beyond their high school community and the larger world. They get exposed here to issues and challenges that before now,

---

[2] www.theatlantic.com/education/archive/2015/05/the-renaissance-of-student-activism/393749/.
[3] www.theatlantic.com/education/archive/2015/05/the-renaissance-of-student-activism/393749/.

they never really felt. These are issues that they can relate to now more easily than they could before. Students organizing on campus for hunger relief issues commented about the challenges others face with finding meals and dealing with how to come up with the money necessary to feed their families. In comments to the media, these students talked about the challenges they personally face economically today with being a working student and how they could not imagine the issues others face because they have even less money than they do.

On college campuses, students can see and study issues far more easily than the general public can, outside of social media. One student in studies about student activism commented, "I would have never known about some given issue that these people were trying to address had I not stumbled upon them in the quad or in the student union building." These students are witnessing their first protests as they walk to class, interact with friends, or grab lunch. The campus is, contextually, a small neighborhood in the global environment, but one that has immense meaning for each student.

The campus has also been a historical site for political and social issue activism throughout history. Students have been at the forefront of many social issues and trying to tip the scales of social movements by spreading more and more information, nonviolent actions on campus, and building a community of like-minded young enthusiasts. These individuals are now also more exposed to policy differences than they have typically been in the past. Again for the first time, they are interacting with issues relative to the reality of the world they now live in and call home here and abroad. The campus itself, too, has policies that for some students represent opportunities for change. Through the lens of political and social activism, the students see change within the campus itself as a global opportunity for change. They remain optimistic that if the campus is able to change and provide students with a new and unique establishment, it could potentially transcend beyond their school walls to other campuses.[4]

This sentiment was echoed in a student from California who participated in an Occupy Wall Street demonstration on her campus. Her participation in several nonviolent protests about economic disparities

---

[4] www.nytimes.com/2012/01/22/education/edlife/the-new-student-activism .html?&uscore;r=0.

was much more about showing with her fellow students, to policy makers on her campus and beyond the potential of change, and that the group on campus was not going to sit idly. She commented that the biggest opportunity for any campus organizing and activism was to be able to show how powerful they could be once they started organizing a concerted effort to bring change to those who hold power.

"People in positions of power, I think they believe nothing is going to happen," she said. "We're just going to yell and scream and hold up signs, and nothing's going to change. But you've got an entire generation of people who realize something is wrong and something has to change because the system is wrong. There are more of us than there are of them."[5]

We can thus conclude the opportunity to work on campus is an ideal one given the environment, setting, and organizational characteristics that exist. Challenging policy or rallying behind a social issue with friends requires support and resources, though, to make it withstand episodic movement building—that is, an investment in leadership to help the self-organized scale up their movement activities.

THE CAMPUS LEADERS

College headlines each year are astonishing, ones like "College Students Raise $12M for THON." From Dance Marathons to Relay for Life, these philanthropic and social movements are sweeping the college scene across the United States. Student groups like fraternities and sororities are all working hard to raise support and awareness for a cause, and national organizations are paying attention.

The college environment is not new to these social movements for good. History tells us that these movements have been in place since the beginning of the college club model when students organized for the support of an issue on- and off-campus. From local issues in college towns to campus policies that need changing, students have long been at the forefront of social movements for good. But until recently, organizations have looked at this segment as "nice"—but not necessarily as a necessity.

---

[5] www.nytimes.com/2012/01/22/education/edlife/the-new-student-activism
.html?&uscore;r=0.

Now this growing population is becoming more and more important given their interest in causes, their abilities to use social platforms to engage in dialogue locally and beyond about a cause, and their abilities to provide substantial financial support for the organizations. One national organization in particular looks to the college youth and young adult segment to raise more than $40 million each year for its cause.

The three largest campus social movements for good (as defined by their participation and financial support) include Relay for Life, which benefits the American Cancer Society; Dance Marathons, which benefit the Children's Miracle Network; and St. Baldrick's, which benefits childhood cancer research. All three provide participants with a combination of activity and fundraising support for the cause. College leaders are recruited to lead the efforts on campus and are trained by national staff members locally and regionally to build armies of more leaders and participants who will enact a movement for the cause. But that is where some of the commonalities start to diminish.

In 2014, my team and I were invited to participate in a private training program for campus leaders of one of the top three social movements for good mentioned earlier. We had the opportunity to attend three days of programming at a hotel outside of Atlanta, Georgia. The national staff brought together roughly 100 of the most successful campus representatives who raised the most money nationwide. Students from some of the largest universities in the country—University of Michigan, University of California-Berkeley and Texas A&M—were all present to learn from one another, compare notes on the latest ideas for raising money, and discuss how they can build a following for causes using social media and other platforms. What we witnessed and learned was inspiring and at the same time very telling about how a group of students can raise more money than some will ever see in a lifetime.

Before attending, the national organization allowed us to send a survey to all 100 campus leaders to try to get to know them. When we were onsite, we were also granted permission to interview 27 of them. These qualitative interviews provided context to the data we received and helped us truly understand the motivations, behaviors, and interests of this group of do-gooders who were responsible for raising more than $20 million collectively. What was fascinating about this approach is that we became able to see what it was that made them so successful in their efforts.

Who Are They?

It was no surprise that the Millennial leaders were involved in their schools. Of the students we researched, 79 percent were involved with other volunteer activities. They had their hands in various groups, including athletics, Greek life, faith-based clubs, and the arts. In fact, about 43 percent were involved in intramural sports, and 36 percent were part of a fraternity or sorority. Approximately 32 percent were involved in a religious organization on campus. Finally, 25 percent were involved in a professional association or club related to their major, 25 percent were involved in their student government, and 18 percent were involved in music, theater, art, or dance.

Approximately 54 percent of the campus leaders worked one or more part-time jobs while raising money for the organization. This compares to the 71 percent national average of undergraduate students who work during college.

Anecdotally, these students expressed immense interest in leadership positions. In an environment in which a leader must be selected, 92 percent said they would submit their name for the position. Beyond leadership, outstanding Millennial fundraisers often preferred working and completing tasks with a team and saw value in delegating tasks. In fact, these students seemed to be motivated primarily by being part of a team and reaching goals with a group rather than individually—building into the movement concept we saw with other movement builders profiled.

> I lost my dad to this disease when I was 12. It's a disease that's really affected my family, and I want to fight against it. I've always been an involved person, so I was thankful for an outlet where I could raise money and actually make a difference.
>
> —Emily, 22

In our past research efforts on Millennials, and in this case, too, we discovered that personal fulfillment didn't come from writing a check. It came from leading and motivating peers to raise money. The joy they received was directly attributable to the motivating part of the movement they created. They relished the meetings, went out of their way to motivate others to get excited about the cause, and found themselves spending more time in the organizing side rather than the asking for money side. This seemed counterintuitive to the concept of leading a movement that raised a substantial amount of money. But to them—that was the success: getting others convinced the cause was something they needed to be a part of. The money, although still an important goal, did not spur their interests.

When Did They First Get Involved?

The college environment wasn't actually the beginning of their cause engagement. Although most of us would think so, it simply wasn't true. Most of them were leaders already in high school. Many all-star campus fundraising leaders got started with a cause in high school (35 percent). Of the students we researched, 27 percent first got involved with fundraisers when they were younger than 12 years old—already embedding the cause interest into their personal interests at a young age. Notably, none of the Millennials we surveyed said they first got involved with a cause after their first year of college. Thus, most of the recruitment was happening at younger ages than as college students.

Their reasons for getting involved differed, but 65 percent of these students said they are involved in the fight against a disease because a close family member was affected. Almost all of the Millennial fundraising leaders had some kind of personal connection, whether it was a close friend or family member or even themselves who were affected in some way. On the other hand, about 23 percent of the students surveyed said they first got involved with their cause because a friend invited them to an event.

In general, our research has shown that Millennials will raise funds out of optimism for a solution. In the case of the national organization we were able to participate in this project with, 62 percent of the individual campus fundraisers believed their work would help find a cure for the disease. For the students we researched, family members played a role in their fundraising success: Almost 85 percent of Millennials said their families were either somewhat or very involved with their cause, with all students saying their families had at least some level of participation—including providing some support for their fundraising efforts.

How Do They Motivate Their Peers?

The students we surveyed and interviewed represented some of the best leaders in fundraising and cause work in the country. Not only did they successfully raise money on their own, they persuaded peers and other students on their campus to fundraise. How did they get other Millennials to raise so much money? What were the best methods for getting high school or college students to join in their event?

In every interview, social media was consistently listed as one of the top tools for putting on and promoting successful events. Every single Millennial said they used Facebook to promote their event and credited the platform as an important asset for communicating with their peers. Twitter was also listed as a valuable tool (77 percent), followed by Instagram (50 percent), and YouTube (27 percent). One group used Snapchat. Snapchat allows users to send images or videos up to 10 seconds long to recipients; once the time runs out, the message disappears.

> We knew that college students were using Snapchat, so we tried to find a way to promote the event using it as a tool. We created an account for the event and started sending people images of posters, people working, anything that reminded them that the event was coming up and they needed to raise money. It wasn't long before people started sending us pictures of them hanging up flyers or sending emails asking for money. It created a community and cultivated some buzz around the cause.
>
> —Heidi, 23

The biggest challenge these campus leaders said they often faced was a lack of buy-in—not from students themselves, but from the staff of the university. A faculty sponsor or a nonstudent staff adviser played a huge role in the success of a campus fundraising event. Whether the adviser was a faculty member or a staff representative from a specific charity, this adult offered a consistent voice and resource to students leading and fundraising each year.

Students who saw the most success in their event said it was because the event was simply "the thing to do" that weekend, having become an inherent part of their campus culture the student body naturally flocks to.

> My best advice for raising money on a campus: figure out what makes your campus tick. Learn what motivates the student body and identifies your campus culture. Is it service? Academics? Career prep? Athletics? Partying? Use your campus culture to connect all students from diverse backgrounds and interests to your charity event.
>
> —**Mackenzie, 24**

Millennials said that videos were essential for pulling peers to a cause. The videos would be original and either funny or emotional, and they would captivate attention, drawing more students in.

To establish an emotional connection to the cause, campus leaders used stories and inspiration. Several of the students said Millennials want to feel that they're actually making a difference, though incentives and competition also work. Many students said turning fundraising into a competition works on their campuses, especially schools with an active Greek life.

> If they leave this year's event inspired, they'll raise money and be back for next year's event.
>
> —**Jordan, 19**

MAKING IT ALL HAPPEN

The trick to Millennial peer fundraising, according to these successful leaders, is to ask your friends and peers not necessarily to give, but to join you in raising money, even a small amount. These small amounts add up and snowball into a fundraising force that can promote and help a cause significantly. Essentially, this became the success equation we were looking for. We discovered that these leaders weren't necessarily the best when it came to asking for money themselves, but they were amazing at getting their peers and other individuals around them to go out and do it for them.

They would organize events, meetings with small groups, and other informal opportunities in and around class to ask people to do one thing—get one more person to give $5. This concept of building a network of askers was the primary role we saw brought to fruition. Essentially, the campus became filled with small fundraisers, all reporting to one another and eventually to the overall leader of the movement.

When we discovered this, we realized that in most of the programs offered by national organizations, there was a deep appreciation for the organization and management of people concept that existed. This is the idea that one person can organize and build an army of people willing to agree to small goals in the spirit of a larger vision. Through the culmination of events and activities that continue to drive the spirit of the concept, the army of askers is not the leader; the leader is a master relationship builder and manager of small groups—the role we see most movement builders for social movements for good naturally fall into.

IMPLICATIONS FOR SOCIAL MOVEMENTS

Social movements can gain traction on campuses because of the structures and network opportunities that exist. Social movements can also gain traction when there is a unique opportunity for students to organize around an issue, garner support from their friends and peer networks, and build connections with resources on campus and through national organizations seeking to build their leadership skills and potential. The social movement builders on campus need a narrative to support a call for the campus community to hear about the issue that can personally affect them—even though they may have been immune to such appeals in the past.

With the campus being a convening ground for social activism, students are conveniently interacting with social movement participants regularly. To build momentum to maintain the social movement each year, investments in leadership will be necessary to help these young activists learn how to continually gain the interest and attention of their fellow students. These skills help them maintain the organizational structure necessary for long-term success in activism and fundraising.

Chapter 9 Creating a Movement ... Bringing 15,000 College Students Together on One Campus

Movement Builder: THON Volunteers
THON, Pennsylvania State University

In 1973, the fraternity and sorority community on Pennsylvania State University's campus came together to dance all night for some worthy causes. Although the opportunity at the time was focused on one or two potential causes, it became apparent that the campus community was on to something. Little did the group of Greek members realize that they created what would be today deemed the largest student philanthropy on college campuses. Today, what is now called THON (short for Dance Marathon) has raised more than $127 million for pediatric cancer research at Hershey Medical Center since 1977, more than $13 million each year, by bringing together more than 15,000 student volunteers from more than 400 organizations and clubs on campus.

So how does this event become a force for so many Millennials on campus to give up their weekends and evenings to raise support and awareness through THON? The answer is simple—dedication, leadership, and highly organized operations at the top. Here's more insight into the model and its journey to becoming one of the most coveted do-good events on a United States college campus.

At the heart of the THON program is the student volunteer. Each year, more than 15,000 students come together to raise money to support the mission of THON—finding a cure for cancer affecting children. These volunteers are organized into several distinct groups in order to reach their fundraising goals. The executive team is led by a dedicated group of individuals who provide a significant amount of leadership time and devotion to the organization. This team oversees various directors based on roles and functions. These directors work with captains at certain clubs and organizations to organize student activation. These captains are dedicated club liaisons who are interested in propelling the THON movement throughout the club environment and build awareness for THON's philanthropic purpose.

Through coordinated communication and trained volunteers, the network of 15,000 students is able to work in unison for the benefit of THON's fundraising goal. These volunteers have an opportunity to organize and customize their approach to raising money. Each club and individual can create events, activities, and fundraising programs that enable them to reach their goals at their own level. Guidelines and support resources are provided to captains and volunteers, but the ideas and concepts are their own—making THON an important self-realized opportunity. Rather than doing it *for* THON, they are doing it *with* THON at their own pace and with their own creative approaches.

What also brings the student volunteers closer and closer to the philanthropic mission of THON is the adopt-a-family program. Through this program, clubs and groups of volunteers can provide emotional support to the families of children with cancer. This type of support, beyond financial, helps the volunteer see firsthand the challenge of the issue. This provides a constant reminder of the need that the students are addressing.

> Our tagline is that we are students taking action in the fight against childhood cancer. Since our inception in 1977, we have raised $127 million for an organization called the Four Diamonds Fund at Penn State Hershey Medical Center, our sole beneficiary. Through our donations, no family with a child who has cancer at Penn State Hershey Medical Center ever sees a bill—all financials are taken care of. That way,

they don't have to worry about anything except their child's treatment and staying together as a family. That's one thing we're really proud of to be able to provide to these families. Last year, we raised $13 million alone. From helping out with transportation needs to basic food and clothing support, our volunteers do more than just raise money—they raise friends and support mechanisms for the families to cope better with cancer.

These families also get the opportunity to attend other events by these volunteers, including carnivals, meet-and-greets, and social activities with students. All of these events help the family understand that no matter what happens, with how much money is raised, they have a group of people who are deeply concerned and willing to be there for them throughout this time of need.

How is it possible these students can raise so much money? It comes down to both traditional and nontraditional fundraising. Some of the nontraditional fundraisers are unique and creative.

First, the organization treats all fundraisers as equal. No matter how much is raised by a group or club, the individuals who raise money get recognition and the support necessary to be successful. The person who raises $25 is considered equally as important as the one who raises $25,000.

Second, a considerable number of students participate in a "canning" solicitation event throughout Pennsylvania, New York City, and New Jersey. Student groups will be on the side of the street, in front of storefronts, and elsewhere raising support and dollars for THON. This is the organization's biggest awareness builder and a big part of the fundraiser's ability to get out in the public to raise support from individuals not within their network. With branded cans in hand, and through thousands of students in and around the areas of the campus, the organization is able to generate great media publicity for the event. This also helps drive ongoing student interest, given the amount of attention to the program.

Third, the organization stresses a multifaceted fundraising model that also incorporates online giving and email campaigns. Corporate sponsorships also drive participation each year, which are typically led by alumni connections.

Alumni connections and relationships tend to help give the organization the boost it needs to reach its fundraising goals each year. Penn State has more than 660,000 living alumni, and the likelihood that they participated in THON is extremely high. Alumni are also parents of current students and become great supporters each year. Alumni passion and interest help drive a considerable amount of money toward THON each year, and with that base remaining consistent and ongoing as students graduate, this built-in donor base is an ideal engagement strategy for the organization.

In the end, though, the fundraising success isn't "that big of a deal," as the individual who heads public relations for the organization told me. The money is just an opportunity to tell the story, even though it provides much of the support the organization receives every year. The mentality of fundraising and the large goal is something that pales in comparison to the meaningful work the doctors and staff are doing with families and the hospital that THON is associated with.

> One thing that we focus on is that the money in the end is obviously a huge contribution but is not as important as supporting somebody emotionally who has a child with cancer. No matter how much money we raise, it's more money than what was going to fight childhood cancer before that. So for us, any fundraising year is a success. That's what THON does and is.

Chapter 10 The Power of Peers

I was in my office answering some emails before getting started with a project I was putting off. As I was about to close my email on my computer, a message popped up from a friend of mine from college. I immediately noticed the email because I code all my friends and family with a particular color to make them stand out from the other emails I get. (I like to make sure to respond to those messages first.)

The email from my friend had the following subject line:

Derrick can you help with this.... it's important to me.

Well, with a subject line like that from a friend, there was no doubt I was going to open it and help if I could. So after opening it, I was immediately drawn to the first line.

Hey Derrick. Listen, this is not what I love doing. You know I hate asking people for things, but this is important and I knew that you would be able to help me.

This was true. My friend never asks for things. He is one of those individuals who keeps to himself and would rather spend hours doing a task or performing a job before ever reaching out to someone for help. Because of his upbringing, he was taught by his parents to never ask for things and be appreciative of what you have.

At this point, not only did he have my attention, but I was also ready to help in any way I could. I first thought the request could be related to either generating awareness about a cause he cares about or something research-related to donors or constituents. When you are known as the "Millennial / research / nonprofit guy" to your friends and social networks, requests like these are not uncommon.

But this request was much different. This email was about helping my friend's fundraising campaign. He was raising money for a cancer cause that I had no idea he was connected to. What I found to be the most compelling part of the message was his story about why he was involved. Remember, he was never one to publicly talk about asking for help or let alone something he was doing to help someone else. So I had no idea of his cause involvement until now.

As I read through the next couple paragraphs of his email, I noticed something right away. This message was heartfelt, authentic, and a genuine request to his friends to learn about and support the cause he was backing. This was not a canned email response provided by a technology platform. It was truly a message from a passionate individual to his friends and family.

Two particular paragraphs in the email popped out at me that are worth noting.

> I am not asking you because I want to hit a fundraising goal or get my name on some website that will recognize me as somehow a hero. I am asking you to help me because you mean so much to me.

> Derrick, I remember when we were in college and you were getting that award for being one of the best. You asked us to attend because it would mean the world to you to see us there. I would have been there regardless. I think this is my "ask" to you—to help because it would mean the world to me.

I saved this email because it was the most powerful message I have ever received from a friend of mine. The message was personal, it had meaning for me and my friend, and it made me feel good to support him. These are the elements I think all of us want to experience when we ask others for support or are on the receiving end of a request. This is the power of peers.

UNDERSTANDING THE ROLES OF NETWORKS AND PEERS

I think almost all of us have been asked at some point to support the interests of our friends. Whether that is buying a product or supporting a social issue, the ones closest to us inspire and influence our behavior. Lately, this concept of influence has been at the forefront of research because of the latest technologies that draw upon our connections and networks more than ever before. From this research, we can understand how the people in our networks take on roles that can benefit the social movements we create.

Robin Dunbar is an anthropologist and psychologist from the University of Oxford. He was the individual who came up with a magical number of real connections a human can have. The answer he came up with, based upon his research, is 150. But how he got to that number may surprise you.

Dr. Dunbar was trying to solve a different problem—one that had nothing to do with the relationships and connections we as humans have. He was wondering why primates spend so much time grooming. He wanted to know why would an animal, even us as humans, devote this kind of time when they could be doing other things for survival. The studies, though, led to Dunbar focusing on the size of social groups.

There was other research out there that described how the size of one's brain determined the size of the social group the individual human or primate would be a part of. This research was something Dunbar wanted to understand the application of when the subject was humans. What is the correlation between the size of the brain and the number of people in our social groups? Through his grooming data and his research methods, Dunbar concluded that the average human, based on the average size of the human brain, can have up to 150 people in his or her social group or personal network. In looking at relationships and connections beyond that number, it starts to get a little hard for the individual to handle. A person cannot process too many meaningful relationships. More people may be known, and a connection may exist, but true social interaction in which both individuals benefit become somewhat limited.

Let's dive a little deeper into the number 150. The 150 number, according to Dunbar, represents casual friends close to us. According to him, the number can grow and decrease. This is best summed up in an article that was published in *The New Yorker* when they covered Dunbar's theories.

> The Dunbar number is actually a series of them. The best known, a hundred and fifty, is the number of people we call casual friends—the people, say, you'd invite to a large party. (In reality, it's a range: a hundred at the low end and two hundred for the more social of us.) From there, through qualitative interviews coupled with analysis of experimental and survey data, Dunbar discovered that the number grows and decreases according to a precise formula, roughly a "rule of three." The next step down, fifty, is the number of people we call close friends—perhaps the people you'd invite to a group dinner. You see them often, but not so much that you consider them to be true intimates. Then there's the circle of fifteen: the friends that you can turn to for sympathy when you need it, the ones you can confide in about most things. The most intimate Dunbar number, five, is your close support group. These are your best friends (and often family members). On the flipside, groups can extend to five hundred, the acquaintance level, and to fifteen hundred, the absolute limit—the people for whom you can put a name to a face. While the group sizes are relatively stable, their composition can be fluid. Your five today may not be your five next week; people drift among layers and sometimes fall out of them altogether.[1]

So how does this apply to today's environment with the use of social networks? Is the number still true today? Is it possible that the average Facebook, Twitter, or Instagram user can manage and connect with only 150 individuals? And how is this possible when so many people have more than that following them and vice versa? I alone have more than 2,000 connections on LinkedIn. Am I truly connected with only 150 of them?

Three studies in particular have validated the Dunbar number of 150 in an online world.

---

[1] www.newyorker.com/science/maria-konnikova/social-media-affect-math-dunbar-number-friendships.

- University of California–Berkeley professor Dr. Hansen and a team of researchers discovered that we have larger numbers of connections through social networks. The connections were not that strong as a whole, but it was with a small group within the total following. That small group represented roughly 150 people.[2]
- Indiana University researcher Bruno Gonçalves looked at Twitter in particular to determine whether or not the user of the platform had deep connections and what was the number of individuals a person could manage. Within a six-month time frame, it was found that users could manage only between 100 and 200 individuals, respectively. And although it is easy to create followings and connections, that range was maintained by all within the studies.[3]
- At Michigan State University, Nicole Ellison surveyed students to understand how they use Facebook. Throughout the studies, it was discovered that the median number of followers was 300, but the students themselves had about 150 people who were really close friends and deemed so by the users.[4]

If we look at social media networks, we discover that people are well connected. But do they truly have a "relationship" with each other? It comes down to how we define our relationships in the online world: whether some of these relationships are truly at a surface level only, or if they represent deeper social connections because they are family and close friends. In reality, the average American uses social media and brings all the groups together. Our closest family and friends are mixed in with our friends from high school and beyond. However, we still communicate the most with those closest to us in those networks rather than those far away from us. It comes down to the true relationships we have with people online and in person.

This brings us to the circles of influence we have within our networks and the power to build social movements by using them effectively. Researchers Liz Spencer and Ray Pahl performed studies on the relationships we have. They focused on the individuals we are close to and the activities we perform with the individuals within each of the circles of influence that represent our network. They found that all of us have eight different types of relationships with people. They are as follows:

---

[2] https://fwb.rickhanson.net/science.
[3] http://journals.plos.org/plosone/article?id=10.1371/journal.pone.0022656.
[4] http://nms.sagepub.com/content/13/6/873.full.pdf+html.

- Associates: the people who don't know each other well, and only share a common activity, such as a hobby or a sport.
- Useful Contacts: the people who share information and advice, who may be related through the workplace and career.
- Fun Friends: the people who socialize together primarily for fun and to experience something together. These individual relationships lack the emotional support necessary for more intimate connections.
- Favor Friends: the people who help each other out for a purpose but still lack the emotional support for deeper relationships.
- Helpmates: this social group of people has the traits of fun friends or favor friends and they help out for a purpose when necessary.
- Comforters: these individuals are similar to the traits of helpmates but they hold and maintain emotional support for the social group that is deeper than just having fun or just being there for experiences.
- Confidants: this group of individuals helps one another, has emotional support, and provides personal information in an effort to help one another. Every individual within the group is a support and also enjoys each other's company through all experiences (fun and non-fun times).
- Soulmates: this group of individuals is the closest to us and represents some of the most connected persons we have. They offer emotional support and can be a force when talking with to buy a product, support a cause, or join a movement.

Product researcher and former Facebook and Google executive Paul Adams refers to the various roles people have with one another as strong and weak ties. These strong and weak ties help influence the individual to act. In his book *Grouped,* he talks about these ties and how the various relationships we have are related.

> Strong ties are the people you're closest to—your closest friends and family. Weak ties are people you don't know well. Often, they include people you have met recently and have yet to form a strong relationship with, and people you know through others, such as friends of friends. Strong ties include our soulmates, confidants, and comforters. Weak ties include our helpmates, favor friends, fun friends, useful contacts, and associates.[5]

---

[5]Paul Adams, *Grouped* (Berkeley, CA: New Riders, 2012).

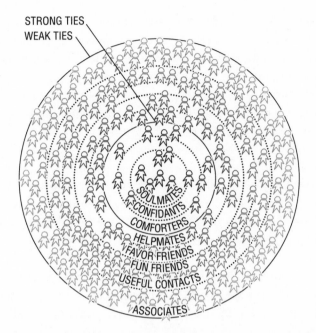

STRONG TIES
WEAK TIES

SOULMATES
CONFIDANTS
COMFORTERS
HELPMATES
FAVOR FRIENDS
FUN FRIENDS
USEFUL CONTACTS
ASSOCIATES

FIGURE 10.1   Paul Adams's Circles of Strong Ties and Weak Ties

He further explains the concept of weak and strong ties through this visual, shown in Figure 10.1.

Adams comments that we have a very small group of friends with whom we have strong connections. If you look across the whole social spectrum of individuals and their relationships, we have the strongest connections to just five people. These are our soulmates. From there we have about 15 very close friends, and 50 good friends. From there our relationships get weaker and weaker as they continue to go further from our inner core of individuals. The real social network, such as Facebook or any other online platform, is a tool to maintain the intersection between these groups of individuals. This doesn't mean, though, that we have the same level of engagement with each group.

Adams further argues that this is apparent from the Facebook data he studied at the time. In his studies of Facebook friends, he further found that users on average have about 150 friends and maintain strong relation ties to five or six of them. The more we like, comment, and post with those friends or soulmates, we are deepening our relationships and further moving others away. It is a form of reinforcement as we deepen the emotional ties we have with people as we communicate with them.

As we look at this research and others, we understand that the peers, those closest to us, have remarkable power to persuade us to act and act on behalf of others for good. These social connections and relationships can be a driving force for any social movement builder to create the peer platforms necessary to amass the public's interest. Given these relationships are present and the social connectivity that exists, we must now explore how to activate them for good.

USING NETWORKS AND PEERS FOR GOOD

Social movements for good need peer networks. The social movement requires a population and peer networks of individuals with social ties to one another. These ties influence the behavior to act for the benefit of the movement and thus result in a powerful force for good.

Involving peers for good requires social movement builders to create platforms of campaigns that serve two primary functions:

1. Perform an act whereby one person can show or demonstrate to his or her network support for a movement.
2. Build the social movement into the individual's everyday life so his or her network can witness the values and concepts of the movement regularly.

In the first function, an individual participates by showing and demonstrating an act to identify with the movement. This is the common approach taken by most social causes and social movement builders. That action may be as simple as sharing a tweet with a social movement hashtag, posting comments in support of a social issue, or taking a photo in the spirit of what the movement represents. At this level, the magnitude of participation can vary based upon one's interests. For example, an individual could show support of the movement by simply sharing information to giving up one's birthday party to raising support for the social movement. In each of these actions, it is the episodic participation of the many that garners the attention of the general public. Combining all of these acts represents the movement to people who are not part of the movement or want to follow the movement themselves.

At the first level, it is important to engage the movement of individuals regularly beyond the episodic participation. This is hard for most social movement builders and organizations that may have started the movement for the sole purpose of awareness building. Social movements that have little ongoing integration into an individual's daily behaviors tend to be forgotten over time once initial participation is complete. Therefore, social movement leaders will need to be mindful of this as they create mechanisms and ongoing actions to maintain relevancy in the long term. Acting can be powerful, but the movement needs ongoing action and participation to maintain its level as a movement.

Marketers of entities that represent movements will need to create a continuum of action that leads the individual to the next step. These actions, in the spirit of the movement's values and beliefs, reinforce the movement consistently over time, resulting in ongoing participation by the peer leader. In the research that we have conducted through the Millennial Impact Project and with other organizations seeking to maintain relevancy, the common issue raised by most movement participants is the lack of ongoing activity and participation. For the most part, these individuals were exposed to the cause and reacted by taking action, but had no place to go once they completed what the movement called upon the participants to do. In retrospect, the individual is already publicly supportive of the movement and has alerted his or her network of such support through his or her participation or sharing, but there are no additional opportunities to reinforce with the network why it should continue to be important.

Building the social movement into everyday life is the ideal environment for social movement builders. This approach sustains the social movement in the eyes of the individual each day and sometimes with each action. This is a consistent reminder of the social issue and tells the network of supporters and friends around them that they care—both in active and passive ways.

An example of this approach to social movements for good can be found more in the social good product world. For example, companies like Warby Parker, TOMS, and Harry's all provide consumers with social models that support the issue they address. This is a clear sign when someone uses their products and advertises that use to the network around them. The (RED) Campaign is another example in which an individual will embed doing good, the social movement and the cause, into their fashion and buying habits. Buying (RED) products and wearing them displays support for the fight against HIV/AIDS.

Changing an everyday habit as a social movement takes time. In looking at the Truth antismoking campaign, breaking the habit of the general population took time and resources. Although effective, this approach may not be ideal for social movements that try to change the habits of the public, which may agree with the social movement but lack the ability to change their buying, environmental, or social practices.

Where we have seen success in certain measures is to tap into the existing habits of consumers and the general public. For example, Charity Miles, created by Gene Gurkoff, allows runners, walkers, and cyclists the opportunity to earn money for the charity of their choice. The individual simply downloads the Charity Miles app, chooses the charity they wish to support, and, when they have finished their run, walk, or bike ride, gets a confirmation of the amount of money they raised. This model capitalizes on an activity this population of athletes was already doing and takes advantage of sponsors willing to underwrite those who want to make a difference. This isn't an episodic opportunity; it is one that takes advantage of the habits of individuals already. Through the app and activity, the individual can share what they have done for an organization and the issue it addresses. This allows their peer networks to witness the power of doing good habitually and consistently.

These two approaches to use peers, through one-time actions and everyday acts, can help inspire a community to come together around a social issue. The goal for any social movement builder should be to sustain the interest beyond these actions to deepen the peer organizer's interest in the issue to motivate him- or herself.

APPROACHES TO SOCIAL MOVEMENTS FOR GOOD AND PEER ENGAGEMENT

Within social movements that use peers, we find that organizations establish two primary roles. These roles include the peer organizer and the peer respondent. These two roles are very valuable to the entity creating a movement for good. Each role has a place within the structure of the organization and is afforded the resources and attention necessary to contribute to the movement.

The peer organizer typically represents the impassioned individual who has moved beyond simple actions on behalf of the social movement to organizing actions and activities for others. The peer organizer has internalized the issue, made it personal, and now devotes his or her own assets of time and skill to making others aware and supportive of the cause. These individuals have been instrumental in building the social movements of today's organizations.

One of the early strategies of charity: water and other organizations such as Liberty in North Korea (LiNK) has been to use their time and energy with marketing and other initiatives to recruit peer fundraisers to build their movements. The power of peer engagement in social movements has yielded incredible returns for many organizations. From the opportunities to raise supporters through raising friends, the power of social movements through peer engagement is a remarkable opportunity.

But what is peer engagement really doing in the space of social movements?

Can peer engagement be the answer to true movement building, or is peer engagement simply an end to the means of generating movement awareness? The answer lies in both the concept and idea of using people to generate other people's interest in the concept of a cause. When looking over the organizations that build and yield significant social movements today, a "self-organizing" model is at the heart of the movement.

SELF-ORGANIZING

Some of the largest movements created today provide an opportunity for anyone to self-organize for and around an issue. How does it happen? This is a common question that comes from marketers and fundraisers as they try to replicate some of the biggest social movements that have existed in history. After careful review of the social movements from 2010 to now, we have discovered several common features and self-organizing techniques that have yielded the highest rates of active vitality through peer engagement.

In looking at the organizations that have created some of the best social movement campaigns, a typical and consistent theme begins with allowing the individual participant to make the cause his or her own. In each case, the individual is allowed to perform the following on behalf of the organization:

- Create a personal message of inspiration and emotion through the auspices of the organization's peer engagement platform.

  In this case, individuals respond to a message by adapting personal experience—drawing emotion and relevance to the beneficiary or issue. This is an important function and allows many individuals to make issues personal—drawing his or her closest inner circles and networks to also respond to the individual's peer request to join them in the charge, making the issue a topic of conversation and the request hard to ignore.
- Create a task for the following to perform.

  In each scenario, peer leaders asked their network to perform an achievable task. This task may be as simple as sharing it with two friends to raising $50. Typically, the most successful peer self-organized campaign involves a peer leader asking his or her network to act not just to show his or her own support but to build support by asking them to expand his or her network to continue the trail of the movement.
- Provide new messages to build new momentum.

  As peer leaders begin to spread to their network interest and action messages, they quickly realize that their audience needs more new and relevant information to keep the narrative of the movement going. They create new messages each week, drawing from new experiences and individuals who responded. For example, as new individuals come on board to support the peer leader, they find that their network has its own story to share. Sharing the individual's story of strength, challenge, and personal experience with the issue provides a basis for the network to constantly reignite its passion—ultimately increasing the sharing potential of the movement itself to more and more people. The peer leader is also a great photojournalist who sometimes creates his or her own imagery or takes advantage of the imagery provided by the organization's resources. Today's peer leader, typically using a host of social networks to spread his or her message, will rely on the message through both imagery and the power of social sharing. The images, new and different, provide a basis for the network to understand the issue's people and support while bringing the individual closer and closer to those fighting for the issue.

- Create a sense of urgency.

  The individual peer leader is great at creating urgency in a time when so many media and marketing messages are simply concerned with informing the individual of the issue. The peer leader strives to make the message timely and relevant, showing the power of why now is the time for the network to take an action because the strength and support of the network is vital and crucial for a short-term outcome. This powerful sense of urgency creates another mechanism and reason for the network to continue the social sharing power by informing the individual of the need to act now even though he or she may have heard the message in the past.

- Celebrate short victories as a social movement builder.

  Peer leaders are masterminds at creating small victories for the network to relish. Through messaging and small, achievable benchmarks, the peer leader is able to create a powerful network of achievers—at least in the eye of the network—as they move from one small goal to the next. Each level of achievement proves a new opportunity for the peer leader to message the audience and network about what is possible when so many band together to show and demonstrate support—an ongoing message necessary when drawing more people in. After such a message of achievement, the peer leader is successful in creating another milestone that the individual in the network would be able to again accomplish. This constant incremental movement building yields the highest rates of response, resulting in more people banding together to reach smaller and smaller goals on a continuum of achievement for the issue.

These are important characteristics to organizing oneself that enables the peer organizer or leader to build an engaged following around the social movement. As social movement builders, it is important to take these characteristics and approaches and develop the resources necessary for these highly engaged individuals to spread the message and narrative of the movement.

IMPLICATIONS FOR SOCIAL MOVEMENTS

Social movements by nature need people. Social movements also need people who will take on roles in spreading the message and sharing the issue's purpose so others can also participate. As people engage their own close ties, we must recognize that for a movement to truly build and gain the attention of the public, we have to help those go beyond the individuals closest to them. We need to provide the resources, information, and tools necessary to make the social movement something to believe in and act upon beyond a one-time action. This is the key to building long-term social movements for good: embed the concept and values of actions into the public's actions each day.

Chapter 10 Creating a Movement ... a Million Supporters and Counting

Scott Harrison
Founder, charity: water

In 2004, a New York City promoter of nightclubs and events was looking for something more from life. Unfulfilled by his lifestyle, Scott Harrison went out on a journey to find his purpose. After a volunteer service trip abroad, he realized that for him, charity was important. Being charitable was an opportunity to influence, support, and help others achieve their goals.

He put his new direction and mindset into motion when he started charity: water, a humanitarian aid organization supplying water to people around the globe. charity: water now has become one of the most admired cause brands and movements in the country. Now, more than 1 million people of all ages have supported water projects through charity: water.

The success of charity: water has a lot to do with Scott's approach to the movement itself—although he wouldn't call their work a movement at all. These advocates see their work as moving people and instilling compassion and generosity. The original concept of his cause work had less to do with a focus on water and more on the concept of helping organizations get the resources they need to be successful. For the first six months, the organization was called Charity. The purpose was to help raise awareness and money for the causes that weren't getting the attention they deserved. Water would be the first cause issue to focus on and then other issues would follow. At the time, Scott thought with pure idealism, he could conquer every single world problem this way. To date, the organization has never left the focus on just water.

He has and always wanted to reinvent charity. He has helped people understand the concept of what charity means, literally and figuratively using the Latin meaning of *love* to inspire how they ignite interest and passion around helping people. With values anchored in less selfishness and greed, he felt the world, if reminded of how important other people are, would build a greater sense of oneself to help those who are suffering.

When he was starting charity: water, he realized there were a lot of people in their 20s and 30s who were pretty disenchanted and not interested in supporting the causes of their parents and grandparents. He didn't see people naturally connecting to the huge multinational organizations working across the globe with lots of money from big institutions and philanthropists. But this demographic was yearning for something—something to be part of a purpose-driven environment. He also understood that these individuals wanted to be involved with a cause when the values of transparency, innovation, design, creativity, and imagination were at the core of the organization. He admired Nike as a brand because it was much more than a sport and clothing company, and was deeply rooted in its values of achieving one's personal best, which its consumer base had gravitated to. Bringing their core values to center on inspiring people and attaching tangible opportunities allows a 6-year-old to a 60-year-old feel as if they are physically making a difference.

It was that approach that led to charity: water being one of the most talked-about organizations in the field of nonprofit causes today. It's hard to go to any conference and not hear about their marketing, design, imagery, and video campaigns that have inspired so many. Their successes in the areas of marketing, branding, and fundraising go back to Scott's view on how causes talk about themselves. He felt at the time, and to a certain extent still today, that the nonprofit sector was stuck in shame and guilt. Showing an 800 number on the TV or computer screen of kids in other countries who struggle with getting the nutrition they need will raise money, but doing so isn't enough by itself, unlike charity: water's imagery of kids being happy and drinking water from one of their wells. Instead, he thinks charity: water is like creating a journey and party around generosity and inviting anyone to be a part of it, where you are proud to wear the shirt of the cause and be a part of something. It's a privilege and an honor to be part of the cause movement. Who wouldn't want to help 5 million people get clean water?

Scott, though, has been mindful that charity: water is not about himself, but about the people who join the movement. Early on in the organization's history, he took a familiar role—being a promoter of the work, his story of why he got involved, and how someone can use his or her birthday as an opportunity to raise support from friends and family. Realizing the hero in every individual who supports charity: water, Scott and his creative team have also shifted to sharing the stories of the incredible people who have done so much for the cause, like the people who climb Mount Everest, the 8-year-old who donates his or her weekly allowance, and the 6-year-old in Vancouver who has set up 12 lemonade stands, all in the hope of helping more people obtain clean water. As he has said, the idea started out as "his story—but now it is our story." It's the story of the fundraiser, the local partner sweating in immense heat to deliver water through a new well he or she is building, and the 10-year-old who just received clean water for the first time.

Scott and his team have also made some significant changes to the approach of how people ask for money. Since the beginning, charity: water focused on the peer fundraiser. The individual who is now inspired to make a difference is willing to inspire his or her closest friends and family. The goal wasn't to go after big supporters or sponsors, which would come later, but rather the person at any age willing to go out and be a trailblazer with his or her friends and ask for support. In doing so, the organization provided resources such as images and videos for the individual to use to be successful. The organization would also allow local partners, not just staff members, to make the ask in materials and information. The organization would help the followings of individuals see the real people behind the wells being dug and those on the ground whom they would be supporting. This is an important approach that is changing the way fundraising is done today.

One of the most powerful moments in the history of the charity: water movement occurred when a 9-year-old girl gave up her birthday party to raise support for clean water. She wrote a personal mission statement that eloquently detailed the reason for her campaign: she wanted more people to have clean water than she wanted birthday gifts. She asked everyone and anyone for $9 in honor of her birthday. Then tragedy hit. Shortly after her birthday, she was killed in a car crash.

People wanted to honor her spirit and generosity. Her campaign took off and more than 60,000 people gave more than $1.2 million. Her story and campaign helped 30,000 lives. On the one-year anniversary of her death, charity: water brought her mom and grandparents to the location of wells that the campaign funded. All captured on video, the girl's mother had a chance to visit Ethiopian villages to see the real people she helped. This empathic response was true generosity in the minds of Scott and his team.

What is surprising, though, is Scott's take on what they feel like they have not accomplished yet. In his eyes, they have had *only* a million supporters in eight years. With so many people around the globe and in the United States, he feels like this number pales in comparison to the number of people who could offer support. He thought they would have a lot more people supporting them around the globe and that clean water would be brought to even more people than what they have accomplished so far. This sense of optimism gives him the drive that he has, the sense that to him, he has not yet cracked the mass population engagement. Although he has seen great success, there is so much more to do, people to inspire, and clean water to be given, that there is no time to let up or forget the larger vision of the organization to help more than 100 million people get access to clean water. To do that will require more and more people around the world to join them.

In the time we spent together, it was clear that Scott is a very humble person. Yes, he is the founder of the charity: water movement and responsible for revolutionizing nonprofit marketing and fundraising, but those things don't really impress him personally. He is still moved by the feeling he gets when seeing a well spill water from its spout for the first time, and the look on the faces of a four-year-old Ethiopian child and his mother when they touch clear water—how they laugh, cry, and show genuine excitement for the work so many charity: water supporters have provided.

Before we left our time together, I asked Scott what he wanted most to be remembered for.

I want the world to remember me as a great husband, father, friend, and someone who lives with integrity. That I truly loved others and was willing to show it every day.

Chapter 11

The Power of the Social Connection to an Issue—Hashtag

If you had asked anyone seven years ago about a hashtag and the power of what it could entail, we would probably all have laughed. But today, the hashtag is one of the most powerful connectors and symbols that have driven social movements to the general public.

In today's digital environment, and in creating social movements, the hashtag is hard to ignore or not incorporate into the social movement building. The hashtag is a powerful symbol showing unity, support, and action by a group of believers in an issue. This is a powerful concept that allows groups of people on a mass level to come together like they never could before.

Some, though, consider the role of the hashtag as a passive form of engagement. Passive it may be, but the power to amass social movements for good cannot be ignored. Let's explore the hashtag and the power it has with social movements.

HISTORY

The hashtag was first used in 1988 in Internet Relay Chat (IC). The purpose was to categorize items such as common themes, images, and discussions to help in the search for relevant content. Users of this

≈ **Chris Messina** ≈ ✔
@chrismessina   +😊 Follow

how do you feel about using # (pound) for
groups. As in #barcamp [msg]?

FIGURE 11.1   The Hashtag Is Born

chat protocol found that by separating keywords with hashtags, they
could easily identify groups of items with the same purpose. This same
approach and role is still active today in social media.

The first time the hashtag was used in conversation online through
social media occurred in 2007 by Twitter user Chris Messina (see
Figure 11.1). He used the # symbol (hashtag) to develop groups of
individual users who could organize conversations online through
Twitter. From then, the hashtag was used not only on Twitter but also
in other social media platforms.

Several years later, Twitter formally adopted the use of the hashtag
as an opportunity to sort, discuss, find, and clarify content strands. The
social media platform created an opportunity for platform users to use
the hashtag by hyperlinking terms and concepts. The Twitter search
engine eventually adopted the hashtag function on its platform. In
essence, the hashtag became mainstream as a way to help organize what
was becoming a very crowded discussion place online. Then, in 2010,
Twitter formally recognized "trending" as a measurement of the overall
activity of a hashtag. Discussions, people, images, and conversations
trend when a significant amount of the platform's users use them in a
short amount of time.

USING A HASHTAG—WHY?

Before talking about the effectiveness of the hashtag, understanding
why someone would use it with his or her social networks is important.
Through our research and in other research by other firms, it is clear
that the hashtag is a form of expression and association. Individuals will
use the hashtag to associate with an ideology and viewpoint. Expressing
the words and concepts of a hashtag to one's followers enables the
individual to project his or her interests on to others.

When an individual perceives that others are associated with the hashtag, it becomes part of one's identity in regard to social issues. The hashtag therefore becomes part of the individual's persona, moving it beyond the role of grouping thoughts for others to follow. Expression through the use of the hashtag becomes the social voice for a community that believes in the same values and ideologies. This results in a social movement online supported by individuals declaring his or her interest, support, and voice to the issue at hand for others to see. The use of a hashtag moves from interest and support to association and movement building—a continuum necessary to amass public participation in the voicing of affirmation or opposition to an issue.

THE POWER OF A HASHTAG

The use of a hashtag can be powerful for social movements for good. Both companies and causes have used the hashtag as a form of connection and awareness building for an issue. The hashtag in a social movement campaign is used in one of three ways:

1. *Expression:* An activist or individual enthusiast for an issue simply posts the words of the hashtag for others to see. This simple action is formulated for expressive purposes for the individual to associate with the movement online and to share his or her point of view within a post followed by the hashtag symbol.
2. *Actionable:* An activist takes an action and captures such action for his or her audience to see by associating the post with the hashtag. In this actionable hashtag usage, the individual uses the post in the social media platform as a way to associate with others through a common action. The hashtag becomes the convening place for the social issue action.
3. *Directed advocacy:* An activist will use a message and a hashtag to direct a post and comment toward an individual or institution to show support for or against the other person's views. This type of social activism through hashtag use enables the individual to associate with others through the use of the hashtag and by amassing a large population directing such statements to the entity or individual, proclaiming that he or she will take some consequential action.

All three uses of the hashtag bring social movement activism to the next level. The use becomes a form of expression, action, and advocacy. The hashtag is presented to a population, individual, institution, or idea. In each case, the actions and expression can be seen by those not associated with the hashtag, with the hope of changing the viewpoint of the minority in support of an idea or issue.

#UNSELFIE

The selfie has become one of the most active social media acts by the general public in the past few years. The act of taking a picture of oneself and posting it to a social media network to share a narrative of place, culture, or personal interest has been taking the Internet by storm. It is no surprise that causes would start to use this pop culture identity action for their benefit.

When an advertising executive came up with an idea for others to take a selfless act of support for an issue, the "#unselfie" was born. This executive created a movement to show support for Typhoon Haiyan survivors—a natural disaster in the Philippines that occurred in the fall of 2013. Within days of the disaster, international aid organizations were using the social media hashtag and campaign to generate attention for the need of donations for the issue. To draw attention, individuals were asked to post a picture of their faces covered by a paper with a donation web address to help survivors. Within days, U.S. State Secretary John Kerry, Hollywood activists, and actors like Mia Farrow and thousands of other people all over the world joined to show their support for disaster relief. The #unselfie rapidly became one of the largest disaster relief campaigns to date. More than 43,000 tweets with 131 million impressions were recorded using the #unselfie hashtag. Stakeholders and global leaders such as Ambassador Phil Goldberg, Jake Tapper, and Bill Weir participated in the campaign with coverage by major media, including CNN, BBC, NPR, the *Huffington Post*, PBS, Radio Télévision Suisse, *Cosmopolitan*, and FHM. And *Preview* magazine featured an #unselfie of actress Anne Curtis on their cover to draw even more attention to the issue, garnering both traditional and digital media integration of the campaign.

Besides being used for disaster relief aid, #unselfie has also been used to garner attention for generosity by the Giving Tuesday movement. Giving Tuesday started as a vision of several key partners, the 92Y and the United Nations Foundation. The one-day campaign was developed to bring attention to the concept of giving back during a very busy end-of-year season. As stated by the organizers of the campaign:

> We have a day for giving thanks. We have two for getting deals. Now, we have #GivingTuesday, a global day dedicated to giving back. On Tuesday, December 1, 2015, charities, families, businesses, community centers, and students around the world will come together for one common purpose: to celebrate generosity and to give.[1]

Since 2012, the Giving Tuesday campaign has continued to garner attention and support for the concept of generosity. In 2014, the Giving Tuesday organizers designed a new hashtag activism campaign by broadening the #unselfie hashtag. On Giving Tuesday that year, individuals and businesses were asked to take a picture of themselves with a piece of paper over their face. On the paper, the individual was to document the cause they wanted to bring attention to in light of support for the Giving Tuesday movement. In essence, the selfie (an act to take a picture of oneself and post on social media) became an act of unselfishness through the campaign for any cause. The results of Giving Tuesday campaigns and #unselfie social media actions by so many people have garnered more than $45 million dollars for causes throughout the country on the day of generosity.

#LOVEWINS

In the final days of June 2015, the Supreme Court was slated to deliver a ruling that would forever change the cultural and social landscape of the United States. The high court was set to deliver its ruling on a case involving the controversial issue of same-sex marriage. The media and the general public were waiting anxiously for the decision to be made

---

[1] www.givingtuesday.org/about/.

FIGURE 11.2   Visa Shows Its Support for Same-Sex Marriage

public. In fact, the court waited till one of the last days of the month to provide the country with its ruling. On June 26, 2015, the Supreme Court ruled in favor of same-sex marriage in the United States.

Within an hour of the ruling announcement, the hashtag #lovewins was tweeted more than 284,000 times. Twitter created an algorithm that placed a rainbow emoticon after an individual posted the #lovewins hashtag. Facebook created a rainbow filter that would be placed over an individual's profile image. This step to show support for the ruling was performed by more than 26 million people. Not only did individuals get into the action of showing their support, but companies did also. From American Airlines to Ben and Jerry's, many businesses began to show social media support for the ruling. Visa, in particular, showed an image of hands joining together with the text "Love. Accepted everywhere." (see Figure 11.2).

The social movement and support of the same-sex marriage campaign was clear through the traffic and attention brought to it through the #lovewins hashtag activism. With such viral attention brought to the hashtag within an hour of the ruling, it can be said this campaign was by far the most widely adopted social issue campaign of the past several years.

#BRINGBACKOURGIRLS

On April 14, 2014, a school in Nigeria was attacked by a terrorist group known as Boko Haram. They had disguised themselves as the Nigerian military. During the raid on the Chibok Government Secondary School, more than 270 girls between the ages of 16 and 18 were kidnapped. Their plan was to sell the girls into slavery for sex. Girls such as these are typically sold into sex slavery for as little as $12.

After the abductions, a Nigerian anticorruption pioneer and social activist, Dr. Obiageli Ezekwesili, started the social media campaign #bringbackourgirls to draw attention to the plight of the girls. Dr. Ezekwesili is the former Nigerian minister of education, founder of Transparency International, and a leader of the World Bank in Africa. As a leading voice in democracy and due process, Dr. Ezekwesili has been critical of the role government should play to help those overcome facing discrimination and dictatorship-type rule.

On April 23, 2014, Dr. Ezekwesili tweeted #bringbackourgirls to bring attention to the issue. The media had not been actively following the story because of other events going on in the world at the time, like the missing Malaysia Airlines plane carrying 370 people. Dr. Ezekwesili continued to draw attention to the abduction by giving a keynote address at a UNESCO event where she asked the crowd to do whatever they could to bring the girls back. Her call to action included spreading the message through social media, holding rallies, and signing petitions for public leaders to see how important the issue is to the public.

The hashtag #bringbackourgirls from that point began to trend globally, drawing attention to the acts of Boko Haram. More than 4 million people tweeted posts using the hashtag. Major leaders, Hollywood actors, and even First Lady Michelle Obama used the hashtag to draw attention to the issue. United States Congresswoman Frederica Wilson led the charge within the American government to bring attention and solicit support for a rescue mission. All of this attention, though, started to fade as both an intervention by the U.S. government and Nigerian authorities became unlikely.

At the height of the social media campaign, the government of Nigeria first denied the event had occurred. The wife of the president of Nigeria went on record declaring that the event may be a hoax to inspire bad press and media against her husband's rule. Later, the Nigerian government vocally expressed support to bring back the girls and find them wherever they are. This occurred more than three weeks after Dr. Ezekwesili sent the first tweet using the hashtag.

At the time this chapter was written, the girls had still not been rescued from their Boko Haram abductors and attention to the issue had lost the attention of the mainstream American press.

#ICEBUCKETCHALLENGE

In 2014, the Internet was crazy with an act that would go down in history as one of the largest social movements to take the general public by storm. By far, the Ice Bucket Challenge dominated the mainstream public's attention for a remarkable two months. What so many were amazed at was the power of the vitality of the campaign to raise support for the ALS Association. How did it happen? What made it such a successful social movement in modern day digital engagement? Some may be shocked to know that the challenge of dumping cold water on one's head actually had little to do with ALS in the early days of the campaign. Let's examine how the campaign began, what made it go so viral, and the outcome as reported by those who participated.

How It All Began

There are several early accounts that a concept known as the Coldwater Challenge was created to garner attention for a cause of the participants. Individuals in Salem, Indiana on May 15, 2014, created a challenge for participants to douse each other with cold water in an effort to raise awareness of a local child suffering from a brain tumor. There were even more instances of a similar challenge created by the National Fallen Firefighters Association and local firefighter houses to raise support for their local charities and those affecting families of firefighters.

These early cases, though, didn't gain the traction the Ice Bucket Challenge did with ALS. The roots of the ALS Ice Bucket Challenge can be traced to the professional golf community. On June 30, 2014, the Golf Channel televised a segment on Morning Drive, a show on the network, in which on-air personalities performed an Ice Bucket Challenge.

On July 15, 2014, golfer Greg Norman challenged Matt Lauer of NBC's *TODAY Show* to an Ice Bucket Challenge—although at the time, the challenge was not associated with any specific charity or organization. On the same day, professional golfer Chris Kennedy challenged his cousin Jeanette Senerchia to perform the challenge because her husband was suffering from ALS. Senerchia's husband had been dealing with the disease at the time for more than 11 years. This was the first time the challenge was associated with ALS. In all other instances, the challenge had been targeted toward other causes or as an act for public discourse. From this point on, ALS became affiliated with the Ice Bucket Challenge.

At this point, the campaign had not gone viral yet. That didn't happen until a man named Pat Quinn, a friend of the Senerchias, started using the concept to generate attention for ALS. Quinn had been suffering from ALS since his diagnosis in March 2013. Since his diagnosis, he was particularly connected with fellow ALS families and other support networks through Facebook. Quinn encouraged his friends to take the challenge; the message eventually got the attention of Pete Frates.

Pete Frates was diagnosed with ALS in 2012. Frates played professional sports. He was a former captain of the Boston College baseball team and played professionally in leagues in Europe. He had a large online community of sports enthusiasts, professional athletes, and ALS supporters on Facebook that connected with his story of struggle and his affection toward helping others, and he was awarded the Stephen Heywood Patients Today Award in 2012. On July 31, 2014, his first posts using hashtags #StrikeOutALS and #Quinnforthewin, coupled with a video about the challenge, started the virality of the ALS campaign. By August 4, 2014, ALS had more than 307,000 new donors performing the challenge. Individuals shared more than 1.2 million videos on Facebook between June 1 and August 13. The Ice Bucket Challenge hashtag was mentioned more than 2.2 million times on Twitter between July 29, 2014, and August 17, 2014.

The campaign ultimately resulted in more than $220 million for the mission of the ALS Association.

Why Did It Work?

This question is often asked for replication purposes. It should be noted that the campaign itself is probably not replicable because of the nature of the setup of the campaign. The campaign is substantially focused on driving attention and vitality through Facebook. It's important to understand how Facebook works to clearly see how the campaign went so viral. In essence, the campaign had all the ingredients for a successful viral campaign on a social media platform that values personal engagement through affinity, posts, and user-generated content.

Facebook is the largest social media network in existence. With more than 1 billion people on the platform worldwide, the network has to create a way to present to each user the most personally relevant stories, images, and content in an effort to maintain interest in the platform, resulting in ongoing and repeat usage.

Facebook created an algorithm, a special code behind the platform, which helps it bring the most relevant information to everyone's newsfeed. This algorithm is based on more than a hundred different factors, but three in particular help define up to 1,500 potential stories and posts in the newsfeed of any user.

- Any posts that come from the closest people to the individual with whom they interact on a regular basis on the platform are likely to get attention in one's newsfeed.
- The kind of action one takes on the content is likely to result in future posts being seen by the user.
- If the post and response are made in a timely manner, the result will be content and posts from a user that the individual responds to quickly.

In addition to these general rules, there are now more factors that contribute to newsfeed viewing. It is important to note, however, that all factors lead to the relationship, the most relevant content, and the user participating actively in discussions and posts.

In looking at the Ice Bucket Challenge, the social movement had three very important factors that led to virality on Facebook.

- *User-generated content:* The campaign featured users uploading videos of their experiences performing the Ice Bucket Challenge. After completing the task, the user uploaded a video. This video indicated challenges to fellow friends and networks present on the social media platform. Because the challenge was documented in the post and called out friends and contacts, it contained the necessary content to get groups of individuals viewing and commenting and taking actions on the content—a necessary win for viral campaign engagement.

- *Timeliness:* The campaign featured individuals challenging one another to perform this act in 24 hours. This deadline made the response time of users called out through the network short and thereby created a viral response movement in and of itself.
- *Challenging groups of people:* The Ice Bucket Challenge featured personal challenges from an individual to other individuals in his or her network. The challenge required the other individual to act by either participating in the challenge or making a donation. Either way, the individual had to respond because of the public nature of the challenge. This response, necessary for the participants, was performed through the network. Such a response, especially from the closest of friends and contacts, helped to bridge the connections among a mass amount of people.
- *The act was compelling:* The Ice Bucket Challenge used a very simple act to draw attention to a cause. The act of dumping ice on someone, extreme for the participant and interesting to watch by the viewer, enabled the act to go beyond simply telling others about a cause. The act was entertaining for friends, therefore compelling others to watch and to marvel at the response of going through the challenge. This enticed viewership in video content from the challenge and on the social network, thus resulting in a viral campaign based on the interest and need of the general public to witness and participate in a simple extreme act. The act of performing the challenge was necessary and at times became the impetus for the population to continue to share, not necessarily because of interest in the cause itself.

What the Critics Said

The Ice Bucket Challenge had its critics. Experts in the fields of philanthropy, economics, and sociology at times lauded the challenge as a meaningless expression not worthy of philanthropy. At times individual activists declared the act of performing the Ice Bucket Challenge as demeaning to the real activists of ALS and missed the point of a real social awareness campaign for the right reasons. Academics also commented on the Ice Bucket Challenge role in pop culture rather than in philanthropy—thus demeaning the importance of the challenge for purposes of creating real change. Even though the Challenge itself had critics, the results were hard to ignore. The campaign was successful in terms of dollars raised and elevating the awareness of an issue most knew little about.

What Can Be Learned

The Ice Bucket Challenge performed and was a social movement that some will never see again in the history of social causes. Replication is unlikely, but that should not be the purpose of studying the movement. The Ice Bucket Challenge had the features of a social movement that others should strive to incorporate throughout the year rather than episodically.

The challenge possesses the key features of a movement that helps make the concept easily adoptable by the general public. The challenge was easy and extreme to perform. Causes typically only create awareness campaigns without asking the public to do something to show their support beyond the money. The act itself was also an opportunity for anyone to take. How many times have causes built campaigns in which the extremism of the act was not possible by everyone?

The challenge possessed an opportunity to bring close friends and family into the act. This is the most challenging action that some causes fail to achieve. The spreading of information and acts for social good require a messenger able to overcome the awkwardness of self-interest in a cause for family and friends. Because the act itself was easy to explain, ignite interest, and gather attention, the state of introducing a cause and overcoming such awkward barriers wasn't in existence. Therefore, the act was simple to replicate on the masses and became the lead for so many when spreading the name of the cause.

The ALS Association needed the Ice Bucket Challenge. The national organization needed the Challenge to bring further awareness and resources to the issue. Although their marketing and fundraising efforts were successful, the ALS Association was not as big for brand association and awareness as other causes such as the Susan G. Komen Foundation or the American Cancer Society. The other medical disease causes had more clout and resources. The Ice Bucket Challenge was the

181

necessary mechanism to elevate the cause without going through the traditional marketing and awareness-building activities so many causes have historically used.

The Ice Bucket Challenge needed the ALS Association. Better yet, the Ice Bucket Challenge needed a cause to attach itself to. By attaching itself to a cause, the Challenge itself became about participating in a simple, extreme action with friends *and* supporting an issue. By doing this for a good cause as described by those we observed and met, it became apparent the cause played an important role in helping others move from watching to also participating. The cause transcended the challenge from a funny and extreme action to a unique and special opportunity for others suffering from a debilitating disease.

In essence, the Ice Bucket Challenge was about people bringing their friends to perform an act. The act itself was unique and a signature action that could be replicated easily with others. Challenging friends to perform, in a public environment, becomes the opportunity that overcomes the awkwardness of just supporting a cause. Organizations should look at the Ice Bucket Challenge not as a mechanism that raised money but rather that raised actions and people in response to close peer network influence. All causes should create an environment in which:

- Regular people can influence one another in a short amount of time to act.
- The act is about the people involved and not for an organization's goal.
- The cause allows the people to own the action, the message, and its delivery.
- The act of supporting a cause can take forms outside of just money—equating activism, action taking, and giving money.
- The result of a campaign is less about the cause winning and more about the people behind the issue, the actions, and the results of the people served by the campaign.

In the end, the Ice Bucket Challenge created a community of people influencing others to act. Although the act itself had elements of pop culture and mainstream interests beyond philanthropic intent, it performed for the cause and generated the awareness needed for an issue so few truly understood. Another perspective to consider about the Ice Bucket Challenge is to question the intent of the movement from those who created it. From Pat Quinn and Pete Frates, who have worked hard to elevate the awareness of ALS, their intent was solely to get others to act in an effort to help more people understand the importance of awareness about the disease. They never met with the ALS Association and conjured up a social movement concept using a challenge and social media. They never worked with an ad agency to create a viral movement that would involve celebrities, including the president of the United States. What's even more important to note is that the ALS Association didn't have in their strategic marketing or fundraising plans a social media campaign that would become a phenomenon. Like any other social movement noted in this book, the Ice Bucket Challenge began with the will of a few who believed an issue that was not very well known needed more attention, and they authentically got others involved. That is a social movement worth noting and learning from.

DOES HASHTAG ACTIVISM REALLY WORK?

This is the big question: Does this type of tactic within movement building really work? Some will wonder if all of this activity generates the solutions necessary to overcome real social problems or whether it establishes an environment in which an individual is passively acting with no real impact. To assess the use of hashtag activism, looking at it holistically is important in the context of social movements in general.

Intent

The intent of hashtag activism is to show one's support for a position on a social issue or to garner awareness in an effort to grab the attention of an opposing group or key stakeholders that can play a meaningful role through their actions. From the participant's point of view, this act of sharing and using the hashtag is seen as personally fulfilling in addition to supporting the movement. Therefore, the intent of hashtag activism can meet the expectation of those who participate, even though the social issue may go unresolved. This is the case with those who share messages online for issues that never gain movement status. The hope and personal interest that is part of the campaign can sometimes outweigh the movement's actual accomplishments.

Expectations

In talking with movement builders and leaders, they often describe the digital attention garnered to the movement itself as a necessary component to the success of the overall social movement. Specifically, they look at digital activism as a component necessary for the organizers of the movement to use when discussing with key stakeholders the breadth of the issue, the interest of the general population, and the activation potential the movement can have on a stakeholder, company, or key partner who engages in the social movement. Therefore, the results of hashtag activism become a necessary component of a larger campaign, but alone it would be challenging to see real change occur. The social movement builders maintain that expectation and create social movements for good that utilize digital and hashtag activism as a representation of the public's voice during meetings with decision makers who can alter the course of a social issue.

Will a social issue be changed by the public's use of hashtags? Probably not without the support leaders provide to take the public's interest and work on their behalf. Social, digital, and hashtag activism in today's social movements are necessary components to show general interest in an issue, and organizers should use this to their advantage. The cause leaders who are successful social movement builders understand the role and maintain an expectation on such actions by the public. But they don't stand idly by while the general population just talks and voices its opinion. They use that opinion to influence the behavior of those in charge of the resources, policies, and decisions that affect the social issues of the general population.

THE IMPORTANCE FOR SOCIAL MOVEMENTS

As we look across various social movements, it is clear that digital activism is important. Allowing people to tag their voice, opinion, images, and profiles for a social issue is self-rewarding and important for the social movement of today. By expressing oneself through social activism and adding the individual's voice to a community of like-minded views, the social opinion of many becomes a social movement. A hashtag message may not be explicitly important in every case, but social movement builders need a mechanism to garner the support of the community for the issue so they can get the necessary policy and infrastructure change to address their need to make it a reality. In social movements for good, banding together by sharing a common message can be the difference between helping a cause and enacting true change. Therefore, social movements need the people to band around a concept and a message–and hashtag messages and activism are perfect opportunities to make it possible.

Chapter 11 Creating a Movement ... Addressing Inequality Differently

Mallory Brown
Founder World Clothes Line

When Mallory Brown returned from her study-abroad experience, she realized the travel bug had not really left her. She spent half of her senior year traveling the world again, backpacking through places such as Indonesia, Thailand, and Southeast Asia. This was a different experience from what she had witnessed in countries in Europe. She saw firsthand the inequalities that existed in the world, like seeing children and families struggle to have food and clothes, the bare essentials we take for granted. She realized that the life she had was much more privileged than most, even though she would be considered by many in the United States as a broke student just getting started in her career.

When she was 24, she started a social enterprise called the World Clothes Line. Her inspiration came from one of her trips. Like so many of us, she brought with her a bag of clothes filled with typical items and necessities. When she encountered so many people on her trip, she realized they needed clothing. It was on that trip that she started to give her clothes away to those who needed it more than she. That was the beginning of what would ultimately become a movement for basic needs in the world.

The concept of World Clothes Line is fairly simple. An individual buys clothes from the website; the company then provides a similar item to someone in need in another country chosen by the consumer, and then Mallory and her team deliver the clothes in person. This model allows the individual to participate with Mallory as a partner and supporter rather than just give without knowing what happens in the end to the person who receives it.

Embedded in the model of World Clothes Line is Mallory's global view. From her perspective, whether you are in Asia or Africa, the issues there affect her as much as the issues in Detroit, where she lives. She is trying to help others see how the world is a lot smaller than people really realize. It is possible through the videos that she produces to help consumers witness the act of giving.

Mallory turned to Crowdrise to start campaigns that could help the families she encountered. But the twist to the campaigns was that she would raise money and then immediately go to work. Her model was to highlight a family or situation in another country, provide basic needs, film the experience quickly, and then return to her donors to help them immediately see what occurred. Using the Crowdrise campaign platform, she was able to tell friends, share the experience with her consumers, and spread the message through social media.

The feedback mechanism of the impact was not typical. As for most campaigns and nonprofit organizations, it takes months to hear back how the individuals were affected—but not in this case. Mallory didn't want people to feel that their money was wasted or forgotten. To maintain the excitement of giving and being philanthropic, she used video and urgency to her advantage.

One of Mallory's first campaigns was for a family in Haiti that suffered greatly during the devastating earthquake of 2010. A single mother named Chantale led the family. She had five children and had to abandon her home and take them to a settlement for disaster victims. Chantale and her younger children were part of the 30,000 families in the settlement that didn't have any clean water, electricity, or proper sanitation. Chantale's oldest son, Jacky, was separated from her during the earthquake, taken by a wealthy family, and eventually forced into slavery. He finally escaped, living on the streets and sleeping in abandoned cars. Eventually, Chantale would reunite with Jacky, but they still lacked the necessities of life to get started.

Mallory and her team created the 86,402 Campaign. Mallory was already on the ground in Haiti when the campaign started. This meant that she would take the money raised and immediately spend it to help Chantale. The campaign started with a $5,000 goal, and in 24 hours, raised more than $10,000. She went immediately to work and videotaped the whole experience, sharing what was going on and sending the video back to the donors. This whole process was so immediate that it sparked more and more campaigns focused on helping while on the ground and reporting back to donors. In essence, donors would give today, and tomorrow they would see how families and individuals were affected.

Mallory is raising money and donors. People she has never met before are hearing about how Mallory can help, and are immediately shown the impact of the gifts that come through and support the families and real people she encounters. The combination of giving now to people while immediately witnessing the power they have to transform lives resonates. Shooting raw footage on the ground to show people what is happening is important and it makes people feel like they are with her, every step of the way, in real time.

Mallory realizes how emotional it is for people to support other people. When connecting a story to someone without the basic needs we take for granted, a natural connection is created. That connection can be reinforced when there is more immediacy in both the story and the response. Engaging an audience to her is not about simply asking and telling a new story later, it is about sharing the powerful role someone can have on someone else now.

Mallory believes strongly that to inspire people, you have to open their eyes to the issues and possibilities. It is not about covering the hurt, but rather the opportunity that exists. For this reason, she has expanded into other issue areas such as homelessness and veterans' issues. Her model of tackling an issue within a 24-hour period, being on the ground and showing the donor how he or she can make a difference can be applied in so many other situations.

Mallory has learned a lot from her experiences so far as a social movement builder. She realizes that she gets the opportunity that most people don't get of being on the ground and being a part of something to witness firsthand. She knows that there are many great people out there who want to be a part of something. When willing to support something, present it in a compelling way, and show immediately what can happen, people will follow. Her comments about her experiences reflect the great opportunity and spirit of a new generation of social movement builders:

> Go out and explore. Take an attitude of fixing things when you see them. Experience them and understand them. Approach things as you want to accomplish them. That will make the world a better place.

Conclusion

In looking across all of the movements and the social movement builders highlighted in the book, it is apparent that the social movements created were less about the organization interested in creating a movement, and more about individuals seeing an opportunity to bring people together for a common goal. That through opportunities such as social media, organizing techniques, and grassroots efforts, social movement builders strive to maintain the core foundation of the movement and purpose throughout—that the movement itself is just an organized entity that represents so many who feel empowered through a common voice and action together.

Here is what is apparent from people who were a part of this book, through interviews, time spent, and analysis. Social movements need threads of connection points today. These threads are connectors, progress, and interest between online and offline worlds. One strategy alone won't work. As much as we would hope for an all-digital or all-offline role to today's social movement building activities, it is not really possible to have one exist without the other. From examples of

#bringbackourgirls to other instances of social movements online that have gone by the wayside, we are now at a point of history, albeit short in nature, that social movements need and require ongoing efforts virtually and in person to be effective.

Movements can't be created just because an organization wants to. This is hard for so many to understand, especially if you exist in marketing or fundraising where the expectation by so many boards and executive leaders is that you will create awareness and, optimally, a viral awareness about the cause and organization. In reality, that can't be manufactured alone or without the interest of the people you represent.

If you are an organization or leader seeking to be part of or even lead a movement, rather than trying to create one ad hoc, you should consider performing the following:

Be with the people you represent in the issue.

This is an opportunity for you to go out and listen, feel, and witness what the people you serve are dealing with. Find commonality among them all. They are the ones who need to come together through you and not for you. Discover the prominent issues they are dealing with that you can't yet overcome without some public assistance. Those are the issue concepts that you can use to create the movement you desire. The best part is that it is real, based on the issues and challenges they face regularly—which will ultimately help you better tell the story of the movement.

Challenge yourself to remove your organization's name.

This could be one of the hardest tasks you will ever find from being a movement builder. The work you are to perform is not about your name, your brand, or the staff or board that you are a part of. Work with the people who need your organization to be a conduit for them to gain public traction and make your organization secondary. This is about the people and the issue, not about the organization. As you create materials, assets, and other external opportunities for public engagement in the movement, help them understand the purpose and act that will tilt the narrative in a new direction. That is your goal. Your work and your organization's name will shine through if you help the individual, the movement participant, play an active role in making the narrative change. They will find value in what you stand for rather than the name and brand you represent.

Social movements need an end outcome—awareness is not one of them.

The best social movements need an actual outcome to point toward. They need to be defined in order to bring people together. Without an end outcome in sight, a common goal that can be achieved, a particular policy, benefit, offering, skill, talent, or opportunity to bring about, the people are likely to lose interest. A faulty social movement focuses on the awareness of the entity rather than an outcome for the people. Helping people come together is not by itself an outcome. Because once together, they need a common goal and output all can rally behind and be a part of.

Ignore technology first—use it as a tool.

This sounds funny given the environment of today's social activist. But for all the movements that have been successful, they have all used technology as a tool and not as an outcome of the movement. They didn't create a viral video just because they wanted to. They created a viral video after they determined what the people of the movement needed to bring them together around the concept and to show the real individuals affected. Technology is a great tool and resource, but it can sometimes crowd our thinking before we can even define what a proper movement is. If you find your board, staff, friends, and family saying to you, "We need to create a viral video," challenge them to talk about the story first and why it is important to the people who will care and join in. Sharing a viral video is a step in a movement to show support; it is not the result of the effort.

Social movement leaders know that social issues require believers to make people act.

In the time spent with social movement builders, the need to find people who can help participants act became apparent. The talent and staff of the organization are great at bringing people together online and in person. The team as a whole is what supports the movement, and every team member has a role in making someone feel as if the movement belongs to them. From the way they answer the phone, to the email they send to a constituent, the movement doesn't belong to the staff but to the people, and the people need the support of the staff in order to make their coming together a reality. Without someone willing and able to support the community and tell their social movement builder or leader that the community won't like this, the movement will fall apart.

Social movements are authentic.

  As Jay, the founder of B Lab and the B Corporation movement, stated, this work is authentic. People can sniff other people out, especially in business and in social movements when the real movement builders are inauthentic. Developing a movement for good is about the authentic challenge people are going through and not the personal motives or the lack of true change that should be the outcome. Authenticity is a characteristic of movements. It is the foundation.

We are wired for movement building.

  It is true, based upon all the great research out there, that the individual has a big interest in this work. We are all wired to be with other people, other humans, to help one another and to truly care when others care, to act when others act, and to respond because we sense others like us may need support. But this wiring to perform can be heightened when a social movement builder can bring the best of our true emotions and passions to the surface. Empathy happens and sometimes could be dormant in our lives, but it is the individual, the peer, and the movement builder that comes along and helps us understand why and how we need to perform in order for our brains to get a sense that others need us.

A movement is what you make of it.

  I was lucky to talk to and get to know the social movement builders who I wrote about in this book. They each have done and created amazing work, and learned how to lead at a time when so many needed such a movement to be inspired from. But anyone can be a movement. Anyone can create change and opportunity. Quite honestly, bringing people together who share a common vision is a movement in and of itself. Nobody I interviewed and talked with had a goal of 1 million people doing something. The number was less important than the concept of just bringing some people together. Movements are what you make of them, and those who come together for the success of a common purpose, should be considered a win.

  Whether you create a movement in your neighborhood with 20 people or with 20,000, the social movements you create—no matter how big or how small—can change the world for the better. Social movement building is an exciting opportunity that anyone who believes they can help bring people together for a common good can bring on. Your real opportunity, though, is the things you will learn from the people and the individuals who share their stories of challenge you are helping to overcome. You will be more fulfilled by the act of bringing people together than the number itself. To that end, congratulations on an opportunity worth pursuing. Here's to the next social movement of our time, and your role in making it a success.

Index